Trying Hard
Is Not
Good Enough

How to Produce Measurable Improvements
for Customers and Communities

Mark Friedman

To order additional copies go to amazon.com
or resultsleadership.org

ISBN-13: 978-1516971626
ISBN-10: 1516971620

Parse Edition 2015
parsepublishing.org

Cover design: Justin Miklas
Interior design: Ross Feldner

To my family.

Preface to the 10th Anniversary Edition

It is hard to believe that 10 years have passed since the release of "Trying Hard Is Not Good Enough." So much amazing work has happened since then. So many new friends. So many new places that have success stories to tell, including extraordinary work in North America, Europe, Australia, New Zealand, and most recently China, South Africa, and Zimbabwe. Plus, there are new resources and tools including recent publications by leading practitioners and the Results Scorecard software developed by the Results Leadership Group.

Some people have urged me to overhaul the book and incorporate the best examples from this new work, but I have not done that. The purpose of this book was never to summarize the state of RBA application, but rather to teach a set of ideas to people who might wish to use them. There are other ways to learn about how RBA is currently being used, including on-line resources like the RBA websites and the RBA Facebook group. What I have done instead is add a scattering of new insights, provide more complete advice about how to run and debrief the crucial Turn the Curve and other exercises, and update references to include new publications since the book's release in 2005. And I have tried to fix things that needed fixing, in most cases a changed word or phrase, a better example or the correction of minor mistakes. (A complete list of changes can be found on resultsaccountability.com/publications.) It is important to understand that there is no change in the basic message and structure of RBA and this book can be used concurrently with earlier editions.

I want to mention just a few of the lessons learned from another 10 years of work. Other lessons will be addressed in the soon-to-be-released RBA Companion Reader. The first is about language. I have become convinced that the lack of language discipline is the biggest problem standing in the way of effective partnerships. This book includes a new and improved "Tool for Choosing a Common Language" which can help individuals and organizations reach agreement on how to talk about the ten basic ideas at the core of RBA. If we could just agree on labels for these ten ideas, we could achieve new and better ways of working together across agencies and across communities.

The other lesson has to do with persistence. Progress does not come in neat forward steps. I truly believe in the power of this work to make people more effective and to liberate them from the useless processes that encumber so many of our society's most important institutions. But there are forces working against us: entrenched older practices, organizational inertia, and fear of change. It is not easy to change the way people think and the way organizations work. It takes time and energy. It takes a willingness to take risks. The good news is that, in spite of some setbacks, there is great progress to show.

Finally there are so many people to thank....all of you who have worked so hard, often without recognition, to make a difference in the lives of the people of your communities. There is simply not space to list the names of all those who have achieved great things with RBA in the past 10 years. I know who you are. I will do what I can to highlight your work. Thank you for your inspiring contributions to the well being of children, adults, families and communities around the world!

I sincerely hope that you will find RBA helpful, that you will share what you learn, and that the worldwide community will continue to grow and connect. I look forward to hearing from you.

All best wishes,

Mark

Santa Fe
September, 2015

Acknowledgements (from the 2005 edition)

Just like every other book you've ever read, there are too many people to thank for this one too. It starts with heartfelt thanks to my mother and father. Their great kindness, solid values and sense of humor helped me become a decent, and mostly functional human being.

After that it's a very long list. Thanks to my wife, Terry Wilson, whose love and encouragement, and skill as a writer and writing teacher made it possible for me to finish this book. Thanks to my sister Janet and my brothers Bill and Ken for their life-long support. Thanks to Lisbeth Schorr, who inspired my work on Results-Based Accountability, and whose groundbreaking work has inspired countless others. Thanks to the Annie E. Casey Foundation and the Center for the Study of Social Policy, notably Doug Nelson, Tom Joe, Frank Farrow, Ralph Smith, Donna Stark, Patrick McCarthy and Ira Barbell who have made my work on this subject possible. Donna, in particular, had faith in this work when almost no one else did and has helped me enormously over the years. Thanks also to Cheri Hayes at the Finance Project in Washington, D.C., and to Judy Chynoweth at the Foundation Consortium for California's Children and Youth for their early and continuing support. And thanks to my very thoughtful and thorough editor, Deanna Zachary. Any remaining problems with the book are my fault, not hers.

Special thanks to Jolie Bain Pillsbury, Bob Pillsbury, Trine Bech, Phyllis Brunson, Susan Brutschy, Caroline Gaston, Mary Lou Goeke, Con Hogan, Phil Lee, Adam Luecking, Jean McIntosh, John Ott, Susan Robison, Phyllis Rozansky, Frances Varela and Becky Winslow.

Thanks also to Yolie Flores Aguilar, Kathy Armijo-Etre, Gerry Aronin, Sue August, Bud Bautista, Marit Bergum-Hansen, Janet Bittner, Mary Brogan, Shannon Brower, Charlie Bruner, David Burnby, Becky Butler, Karin Callaghan, Sue Cameron, Jo Cavanagh, Pat Chaulk, Ira Cutler, Anna Danneger, Libby Davies, Judy DeBarros, Lynn DeLapp, Lori Dobkins, Paula Duncan, Lynn Fallin, Reyna Farales, Tim Farland, Theresa Fujiwara, Sid Gardner, Melissa Gibson, Andy Gill, Alfreda Gonzales, David Gray, Curtis Haats, Lena Hackett, Jamie Halpern, Gail Hayes, Bill Herman, Jono Hildner, Gail Hobbs, Sara Hoffman, Rob Hutchinson, Kelly Hyde, Jann Jackson, Scott Johnson, Jana Jones, Dennis Kane, Aliya Kedem, Pat Kelly, Susan Kelly, Judy Langford, Beth Leeson, Chris Linville, Janice Lovegrove, Gerry Maher, Thijs Malmberg, Deena Margolis, Kathy Martin, Howard Mason, Ruth Massinga, Jacqueline McCrosky, Thea Meinema, Linda Miller, Cheryl Mitchell, Sammy Moon, Caroline Moore, David Murphey, Judy Nelson, Liz O'Dell, Maria

Elena Orrego, Janice Parks, Magda Peck, Mike Pinnock, Sheila Pires, Donna Podrazik, Miriam Podrazik, Tim Reardon, Steve Renne, Connie Revell, Sue Richards, Julie Sapp, Don Schmid, Stan Schneider, Ken Seeley, Phyllis Sherard, Anita Siegel, Barbara Squires, Gary Stangler, Bob Stoughton, John Sullivan, Keith Sykes, Theresa Tanoury, Kathy Tucker, Khatib Waheed, Diana Wahle, Sara Watson, Susan Williamson, Richard Wood, and Patricia Zuluagar.

Thanks to the many many other wonderful friends and colleagues who have been such great partners in this work and who have taught me so much over the years. I wish I could print all of your names here, and give recognition to all of your accomplishments, but you know who you are, and I know who you are. Thank you.

About the Author (2015)

Mark Friedman has over four decades of experience in public administration and public policy and the scars to prove it. After one year as a high school math teacher, he worked 19 years for the Maryland Department of Human Resources, including six years as the Department's Chief Financial Officer. After leaving state service he spent four years with the Center for the Study of Social Policy in Washington D.C., and then 19 years as founder of the Fiscal Policy Studies Institute. That's 43 years if you were counting. Mark has published a wide range of papers on Results-Based Accountability and other topics and has spoken extensively across the US and around the world. He lives with his wife Terry in Santa Fe, New Mexico, too far away from his much loved children, Megan, Julie, and Aaron, and grandchildren, Mikayla, Carson, Bolton, Taylor, Tashi, Zachary and Sonam.

Contents

Prologue[1]

If you picked up this book, you have probably wasted hours perfecting mission statements, filled out page after page of logic model forms, or compiled reams of reports that nobody used. You have been frustrated by "experts" acting superior while talking in complete gibberish. You have endured endless management meetings and community meetings that wasted your time with all talk and no action. Perhaps you have worried that these processes were wasting something more important than time; that they were wasting people's passion and willingness to work hard for an important purpose.

This book is about a different way. It is about getting from talk to action quickly. It provides a method of thinking and taking action together that is **simple** and **common sense,** that uses **plain language**, produces **minimum paper** and is actually **useful** to community members, managers and decision makers. It is about making a difference, not just trying hard and hoping for the best. The Results-Based Accountability (RBA) framework[2] presented in this book can be used to improve the quality of life in communities, cities, counties, states and nations, including everything from the well-being of children to the creation of a sustainable environment. It can help government and private sector agencies improve the performance of their programs and make them more customer-friendly and effective. RBA is a common sense approach that replaces all the overly-complex jargon-laden methods foisted on us in the past. The methods can be learned and applied quickly, and all the materials are free for use by government and non-profit organizations.[3]

This book is written for several different audiences. The first several chapters are written for the general public. Later chapters are somewhat more technical and are written for practitioners who wish to implement these ideas. The early chapters are easy to read, although not quite beach reading. The later chapters are a little more like a textbook.

---

1. If you object to reading this first section, you must be anti-logue.
2. The framework in this book has been known by at least four different names: Results-Based Accountability™ (RBA), Outcomes-Based Accountability™ (OBA), Results and Performance Accountability, and Results Accountability. The name "Outcomes Based Accountability" is widely used in the UK and some other parts of the world. The name "Results-Based Accountability", or RBA, has become the most common name and is used throughout the book. Unfortunately, it's too cumbersome to always refer to both names.
3. And small for-profit consulting firms. See the notice at the end of Chapter 9 for details.

Chapter 1 provides a summary of all the basic ideas of RBA. You can read this chapter in about 5 minutes and put the book back on the shelf. You can probably do this in the book store and not even pay for it.

Chapter 2 sets out easy-to-understand definitions for the most important ideas in the book and then explains the basic RBA talk-to-action thinking process. The explanation is in the form of a Socratic dialogue about how to fix a leaking roof, taken from Plato's popular series on home repair. Then we talk about the two components of the RBA framework: Population Accountability, addressed in Chapter 3, and Performance Accountability addressed in Chapter 4.

Chapter 3 presents Population Accountability and how to get from talk to action on the well-being of the people in a community, city, county, region, state or nation. For example, we want children to be ready for school and successful in school. We want their parents to have living wage jobs. We want to live in safe communities with a clean environment. We call these conditions of well-being "results." The chapter describes how to identify the most important results, pick the best measures, and agree on the most powerful actions that will make things better, including no-cost and low-cost actions.

Chapter 4 presents Performance Accountability and how to get from talk to action on the performance of programs, agencies and service systems. First we discard the industrial input-output jargon and talk about people as change agents, not parts of an organizational machine. Then we identify the world's simplest yet complete way to categorize performance measures: *How much did we do? How well did we do it? Is anyone better off?* The chapter describes a 45 minute (not weeks, months or years) method to pick the most important measures for a program, and 7 questions that every manager can use to improve their program's performance. This is "get to the point planning." Set aside your work on the perfect mission statement and begin using performance measures right away to improve performance.

Chapter 5 shows the relationship between Population and Performance Accountability. Population results are a matter of collective accountability, not the job of any one program. Programs are accountable for helping their specific customers, not for changing the entire community. Programs contribute to community results by helping their customers.

Chapter 6 addresses what happens when management, budgeting and strategic planning systems operate as disconnected parts of an organization. RBA makes it possible to turn these separate systems into a single system. This chapter includes an approach to simplifying school improvement planning. It also provides a common sense way for foundations, United Ways and other funders to use RBA to make grants.

Chapter 7 addresses how to bring people together to do this work and offers some tools that can help, including a tool for choosing a common language and a results-based agenda for meetings. This chapter also describes a new way to show whether programs and community change processes are working. The chapter compares RBA to other frameworks and calls for the creation of a consumer's guide for management and planning models.

Chapter 8 wraps things up. RBA can change how we think and how we work together. It can be used to measurably improve the quality of life in our communities and the performance of our programs. In the thrilling conclusion we envision 1,000 communities and 1,000 programs using these common sense methods to make things better. The reader is invited to join the growing community of people around the world using RBA.

Chapter 9 is a virtual chapter, consisting of two websites. The first website, **raguide.org** is an implementation guide for RBA organized around questions that people typically ask about this work, such as "What do we do if we don't have any good data at all?" The site also has numerous additional tools, case studies and links to important sites. The second website, **resultsaccountability.com** is the home of the Fiscal Policy Studies Institute, with papers about RBA and related topics, links to other resources, and a terrific recipe for green chile stew.

If you want, you can read the book from beginning to end as you would any other book. Or you can skip around to the sections that interest you. If nothing in the book interests you then send a complaint to the Fiscal Policy Studies Institute, attention Complaints Department.

Please be warned that there is some humor in this book that is only slightly related to the topic at hand. Humor is an enormously important part of life, particularly when it comes to deadly serious topics like improving the lives of children and families, planning, budgeting, and performance measurement. So look for this book to not take itself too seriously all of the time.

Introduction

My first year out of college, I worked as a high school math teacher. It was the hardest job I ever had, twenty-four hours a day of teaching, thinking about teaching, and dreaming about teaching. I only lasted one year, which is a source of embarrassment as I meet dedicated teachers who have made this their life's work. But I remember my students and what it felt like to be alone in that classroom trying to make a difference in their lives.

After teaching, I spent the next 19 years working for the Maryland Department of Human Resources, the department responsible for welfare, food stamps, child welfare, child support enforcement, energy assistance and many other social services. I worked my way up to be the Assistant Secretary for Planning and Evaluation and the Department's Chief Financial Officer. I learned a lot about how important decisions get made in the real world and it wasn't always pretty. It was about mostly good and some not-so-good people in a world of politics, press, pressure, and not enough money. We did a lot of things right and made our share of mistakes.

One of the mistakes we made was to try to implement the Program Planning and Budgeting System (PPBS). This was all the rage in government in the late 1960's and early 1970's, coming downstream from the Lyndon Johnson administration. This was a time when the states viewed the federal government as a source of new ideas. The only problem with PPBS was that it didn't work. We spent thousands of hours producing a beautifully bound seven volume set of plans that went up on the bookshelf. No one looked at the plans again until the next year when we had to produce the next seven volume set, a complete waste of time.[4]

In 1991, I left state government and went to work in Washington D.C. with a small non-profit think tank called the Center for the Study of Social Policy (CSSP). Most people believe that a think tank consists of people with their feet up on the desk thinking, or perhaps people thinking in an armored vehicle, or immersed in a tank of water, but that's not what it was. We had to work with people who were trying to improve the lives of children and families in their community, and then write scholarly papers about what we learned.

[4.]   There is only one state in the U.S. that still uses PPBS. They wrote PPBS into state law and no one seems to know how to get rid of it.

One day in my second year at the Center, I got a chance to travel to Rochester, New York with Lisbeth (Lee) Schorr, author of the groundbreaking book *Within our Reach: Breaking the Cycle of Disadvantage*. We spoke to the Rochester 90 Day Committee, so named because they were all told they would finish their work on community well-being in 90 days. It was a ruse to get good people to commit their time and it worked. We were there well past day 91. At the time, I was teaching people about financing children's services and how to get more federal money to support their programs.[5] The problem was that people rarely had any established plan for how to use the new money, they just wanted me to tell them where it was buried. That was a problem because without a commitment to reinvest the money, it was almost always taken away and used for something else that had nothing to do with children and families. This left programs worse off than they were before, having a lot more paperwork to do (Medicaid claims produced by schools, for example) and no new money to show for it. This made me a passionate advocate for getting a binding reinvestment commitment before any actual refinancing work was done.[6] My charge for the day was to tell them where the money was buried and urge them to get a reinvestment agreement. Lee was there to talk with them about "outcomes."[7]

I had never heard anyone talk about outcomes before. I had used that word many times, but never in the way Lee was suggesting. She was talking in plain English about outcomes as conditions of well-being for children and families, like *Safe Children* or *Children Ready for School*, and how you could "un-bundle" these outcomes into component pieces that could be measured. Measures could then be used to assess progress. It wasn't about more money for more programs, but stepping back and thinking about the purpose of our work together and beginning a disciplined process of making things better. It suddenly made sense of things I'd been thinking about for a long time.

I went back to my office and, in genuine think tank style, with my feet on the desk, began to think "What if we were serious about Lee's outcomes? What if it really mattered if children were ready for school, if families had sufficient income to raise their children, or communities were safe? What if it really mattered if we succeeded or failed? What would we do differently? And in particular, what would I, as a fiscal officer, have done differently in my previous job?" All of the work that has followed, including this book, is an answer to that single question: **"What would we do differently if outcomes really mattered?"**

Lee's outcomes seemed like the right place to start. If we knew what outcomes we wanted and how to measure them, the next logical thing to do would be to assess ex-

---

5. See "The Cosmology of Financing" on resultsaccountability.com under FPSI Publications.
6. Reinvestment commitments should be obtained even before there is a formal estimate of how much money might be generated. There are several instances where money was taken away based on estimates. In at least two states an amount equal to the estimated Medicaid reimbursement was removed from the schools' formula funding, on the assumption that the schools would replace it when they processed the Medicaid claims.
7. The word "outcome" and "result" are used interchangeably in this section.

actly how we were doing on each of the measures. We would then forecast, as fiscal people are wont to do,[8] whether things were likely to get better or worse if we just kept doing what we were doing. We would dig into what was causing conditions to get better or worse. We would think about partners who might help us do better, and what works to do better. Out of all this thinking, we would decide on an action plan and get started. This is what fiscal people do. This is what business people do. This is what military people do. This is what athletes and managers do. This is what all successful people do. So why weren't we doing it?

There are many reasons why the great majority of social enterprises, whether public or private, don't work this way. I believe the main reason is a culture of defeatism that pervades the public and non-profit sectors of our society. It goes like this: "These problems are so big and complicated, there's no way my program is going to make more than a small dent. Why be ambitious? I will work in my little corner of the world and try hard. And if I try hard, at least I can sleep at night knowing I've made a small difference." If a business executive did this, the business would fail. If a general in the field did this, the military campaign would fail. And so when we come face to face with difficult social problems, we take on this attitude, and we almost always fail. As you may have guessed from the book's title, this kind of trying hard is not good enough. There has to be a better way.

I am not the first person to see this problem and try to solve it. There is a long history of innovation in management, budgeting and planning, and many before me have made important contributions to this work. What I began to see after the trip to Rochester was that these previous methods didn't seem to work well when the stakes were very high. Almost any planning method can be used to raise money and build a recreation center. However, the methods don't work so well if the task is turning around teen pregnancy, juvenile crime, environmental decline or poverty.

There was another dimension to this problem that I began to understand after Lee's session. Fixing the formal system of government and non-profit services is not the same thing as improving the quality of life for children and families. We could get the service system spinning like a top, while overall conditions for children and families got worse. In fact, this is exactly what was happening. We were pouring billions of dollars into social programs that claimed to be successful, and could demonstrate significant benefits, but overall social conditions for children and families were getting worse. **How is it possible to have all these successful programs while conditions get worse?**

The answer to this paradox requires stepping outside the service delivery system and looking at population well-being as something bigger than programs, bigger than agencies, and indeed, bigger than government itself. This is hard for people in the service system to do. When you are working for a particular agency, your worldview is

---

8.   Surplus / deficit forecasting is among the most important things fiscal people do. If you forecast a deficit you have no choice but to act, unless you're the federal government.

bounded by the edges of the services you deliver. And there are dozens of little fiefdoms - health care, education, child welfare, juvenile justice, mental health, public safety, economic development, transportation, and the environmental protection system - each with its own bounded view of the world, each thinking that if only someone would provide enough money to do everything that needed to be done, some big problems in society could be fixed.

This is the number one excuse that honest, creative, well-meaning people in government use to feel OK about giving up. "If we had enough money we could fix it. 'They' will never give us the money we need. So it will never be fixed and it's not our fault." It's a brilliant, self-contained, self-perpetuating, view of the world that says, not only is trying hard good enough, it's the only thing there is. The solution to improving quality of life conditions for our children and families, for our communities, cities, counties, states and nations cannot and does not lie solely in the system of formal government and private sector services. This does not mean that government and private sector spending is not important. Quite the contrary. Government investments are an essential part of any solution, but they can only be part of the solution, not the whole.

A few years ago, in preparing for a speech about child welfare reform for a leadership group in California, I discovered an analogy that helps explain this perspective. Do you remember the television show MASH? The hospitals portrayed in that show were treating the casualties from the Korean War. Our government programs for child protection are just like MASH units. They treat the casualties from the wars that go on in the families in our society. No one expected the MASH units to end the Korean War and no one should expect child protection programs to end child abuse. We can expect child protection programs to do the best possible job with the children who come to their attention. However, ending, or significantly reducing child abuse will take many more players than just child protection services.

Think for a minute about all the potential partners in your community who might have a role to play in reducing child abuse: parents, churches, doctors, hospitals, schools, police, the business community, the media. We could create quite a long list. The same applies to getting all children healthy. It's not just the Health Department's job. Economic prosperity is not just the responsibility of the Economic Development agency. Safe roads require more than just the Department of Transportation, and a clean environment demands more than just the Department of the Environment.

If ending or significantly reducing these problems is not within the reach of public and private sector programs and agencies, what is the role of programs and agencies at all? The answer lies in the profound difference that exists between **programs** and **populations**. Programs must do the best possible job improving the lives of their customers, those directly served by the program. For populations, we must create the community, city, county, state and national partnerships necessary to make progress for people, whether they are receiving services from programs or not. These are separate but connected efforts and we must do **both** of them well. Now this may sound obvious. It may be the professed belief of many in the system. But it is not how we act.

Fast forward. What happens when you hold a public agency accountable for population conditions of well-being? Consider the case of a health department that defined one measure of their agency performance as follows: "The rate of low birth-weight births will be less than 5% of live births." There are actually two things wrong with this. The first is that they placed a standard (5%) directly into the measurement statement itself.[9] By defining success this way, they effectively ruled out recognition of incremental progress (e.g. going from 7% to 6%) and set themselves up for failure. The more important mistake was taking a **population** measure (rate of low birth-weight births) and using it as a **program performance** measure for their agency. In a single stroke, their agency assumed sole responsibility for bringing this number below 5%, with no mention of the role of any other partners. So every month the population rate was not below 5%, they were getting beaten up in the press for the poor **performance of their agency**, and wondering why.

After enough beatings, reasonable people retreat to the bunker of "bunker mentality" fame. This same problem was created by the Government Performance and Results Act (GPRA) in 1993, when the United States Congress failed to recognize the difference between Population and Performance Accountability and bunkers sprouted all over the place.

What we need is a system of thought and action that allows population well-being and the performance of programs and agencies to be treated as separate but connected enterprises. That is what this book is about: how to do both well and how they are connected.

After leaving the Center in 1996, I formed the Fiscal Policy Studies Institute to pursue these questions. Since then I have presented the RBA framework to thousands of people around the world, in national, state, county and city governments, in United Ways, school districts, tribal governments, non-profit organizations, charitable foundations and neighborhood associations. The framework has been used in over 40 states in the US and many other countries including Australia, Canada, Chile, China, Ireland, Israel, Qatar, Luxembourg, the Netherlands, New Zealand, Norway, South Africa, Sweden and the U. K. I have had the good fortune to travel to interesting places and work with wonderful people. This book is a compilation of 10 years worth of insights gained from these travels. I have come to believe that this work is unique in many ways, but most importantly, it meets the tests I posed at the beginning of the book: simple, common sense, plain language, minimum paper and useful. Whatever other methods you may be using, hold them up to these five standards and see how they rate. If you are perfectly satisfied, then set the book aside and keep on with what you're doing.

---

9. See Chapter 4, using data to compare performance and set targets without creating fear of punishment.

A word or two about the stories in this book. The stories here are all true. Where a story shows a place in a favorable light, the place will be named. But where the story is not complimentary, the name will be withheld. The rare exception is where I think naming the place may actually help solve the problem. This may be frustrating, but it is my way of honoring the trust that people have placed in our work together.

A word about acronyms and jargon. Acronyms and jargon are ways of excluding people by talking in a way where only some people know what is being said. If we want these processes to be inclusive, we need to use inclusive language that everyone can understand. Apart from the acronym "RBA," I have tried to avoid the use of acronyms and jargon,[10] to say things in plain everyday language as much as possible. However, it is inevitable that the process of talking about new ideas will require new ways of using words and phrases, so forgive me if I occasionally fail to use the clearest language.

Finally, a word about the program and community examples in this book. Everyone has to come from somewhere. My background is in working with family and children's services, including social services, education, health, mental health and juvenile justice. But the concepts in this book can be applied to any field of government or non-profit work, and indeed to for-profit organizations as well. Since founding FPSI, I have worked with just about every part of the government and nonprofit sector, including departments of environment, transportation, economic development, police, water and sewer, and fish and game, in addition to child and family social services. I have worked with both the executive and legislative branches. And I have worked with population conditions that span the distance from children ready for school to national security. While many of the examples given here come from health, education and social services, I believe you will quickly see the applicability to whatever kind of work you do.

---

10.   As part of the Anti-Acronyms and Jargon Campaign, or AAJC.

Chapter 1:

WHAT IS RESULTS-BASED ACCOUNTABILITY (RBA) AND HOW DOES IT WORK?
(All the basic ideas in 5 minutes)

What is it? Results-Based Accountability (RBA) is a disciplined way of thinking and taking action that can be used to improve the quality of life in communities, cities, counties, states and nations.[11] RBA can also be used to improve the performance of programs[12], agencies and service systems.

How does it work? RBA starts with ends and works backward, step by step, to means. For **communities**, the ends are conditions of well-being for children, adults, families and the community as a whole such as *Residents with Good Jobs, Children Ready for School, A Safe Neighborhood, A Clean Environment* or even more specific conditions like *Public Spaces without Graffiti* and *A Place Where Neighbors Know Each Other*. For programs, the ends are how customers are better off when the program works the way it should such as the percent of people in a job training program who get and keep good paying jobs.

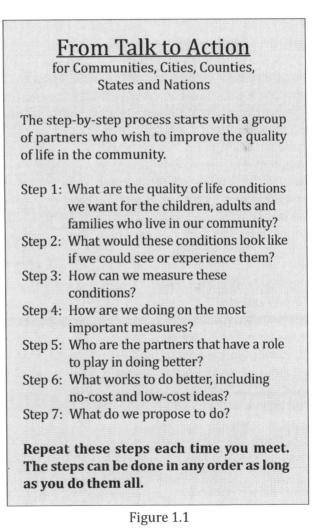

From Talk to Action
for Communities, Cities, Counties, States and Nations

The step-by-step process starts with a group of partners who wish to improve the quality of life in the community.

Step 1: What are the quality of life conditions we want for the children, adults and families who live in our community?

Step 2: What would these conditions look like if we could see or experience them?

Step 3: How can we measure these conditions?

Step 4: How are we doing on the most important measures?

Step 5: Who are the partners that have a role to play in doing better?

Step 6: What works to do better, including no-cost and low-cost ideas?

Step 7: What do we propose to do?

Repeat these steps each time you meet. The steps can be done in any order as long as you do them all.

Figure 1.1

---

11. The word "community" will be used as a shorthand for people who live together in a geographic area, including the whole range from neighborhoods to nations.

12. For readers in the EU, Australia and New Zealand, the term "program" will be used throughout the book to mean "service."

How can it help? Many people have been frustrated by past efforts that were all talk and no action. RBA is a process that gets you and your partners from talk to action quickly.

It uses plain language and common sense methods that everyone can understand. The most basic version of RBA can be done in less than an hour and produces ideas that can be acted on immediately. (See the Turn the Curve exercises in Appendix E.) RBA is an inclusive process where diversity is an asset and everyone in the community can contribute. Like all meaningful processes, RBA is hard work. But it is work that you control and that makes a real difference in peoples' lives. Figure 1.1 shows the talk-to-action 7 Questions for communities, cities, counties, states and nations. Figure 1.2 shows the talk-to-action 7 Questions for programs, agencies and service systems.

The RBA thinking process.

We all use the thinking process behind RBA to solve problems in our lives. Have you ever had a leaking roof? You know it's leaking when you see water dripping down. To fix the leaking roof, you think about who could help you. Then someone has to get up on the roof and figure out why it's leaking. Next you think about how it could be fixed. And finally you decide what you will actually do to fix it. You know it's fixed when you stop seeing water. This sequence gets a little more complicated when you're trying to "fix" conditions in your program or community, but the RBA steps come from this same way of thinking.

An action plan after the first meeting.

People often give up on community change processes because of confusing language and lack of action. You go to a meeting and everyone is talking in jargon. You feel excluded and you don't come back. Or, you go to a series of meetings and nothing happens. You feel bored and frustrated and you don't come back. RBA is a process that uses plain language and where there are actions to take after the first meeting.

From Talk to Action

for Programs, Agencies and Service Systems

The step-by-step process starts with a manager or group of managers who care about the quality of their services.

Step 1: Who are our customers?

Step 2: How can we measure if our customers are better off?

Step 3: How can we measure if we're delivering services well?

Step 4: How are we doing on the most important measures?

Step 5: Who are the partners that have a role to play in doing better?

Step 6: What works to do better, including no-cost and low-cost ideas?

Step 7: What do we propose to do?

Repeat these steps each time you meet. The steps can be done in any order as long as you do them all.

Figure 1.2

Why is data important?

When you're trying to fix a leaking roof, you don't really need data. You can see if the roof is leaking or not. But community conditions and the way programs work are much more complicated. If we rely on just impressions and anecdotes, we don't really know if things are getting better or worse. By using common sense measures, we can be honest with ourselves about whether or not we're making progress. If we work hard and the numbers don't change, then something more or different is needed. We rarely have all the data we need at the beginning, but we can start with the best data we have, and get better data. Data doesn't always have to be gathered by the experts. You can use simple, common sense methods, like community surveys with just a few questions, or a walking count of vacant houses each month, or even a show of hands at the monthly meeting about how many people know someone who was a crime victim in the last 30 days.

Why is common language important?
Whether it's English, Spanish or another language, we often use words in confusing ways that no one really understands. People who work together need a common language to be successful. RBA asks groups to agree on what words they will use to describe a few basic ideas:

Results: The conditions of well-being we want for our children, families and the community as a whole.

Indicators: How we measure these conditions.

Baselines: What the measures show about where we've been and where we're headed.

Turning the curve: What success looks like if we do better than the baseline.

Strategies: What works to improve these conditions.

Performance measures: How we know if programs and agencies are working. RBA uses three common sense performance measures: *How much did we do? How well did we do it?* and *Is anyone better off?*

Where has RBA worked?
RBA is being used across the United States and around the world. There is a growing network of people with success stories to tell. Some of these stories are presented in the sections between chapters. In Vermont, state and local partners turned the curve on a wide range of measures including blood lead levels in young children, child abuse rates and high school dropout rates. Santa Cruz County, California turned the curve on teen alcohol and drug use. Montgomery County, Ohio turned the curve on school attendance rates. California, Maryland, North Carolina and other states and counties are turning the curve on the percent of children ready for school. State and local governments, school districts, non-profits and tribal governments in Arizona, Connecticut, Hawaii, Idaho, Oklahoma, Kentucky, Michigan, Minnesota, Washington, and many other places around the world have used RBA to improve the performance of their programs and agencies.

What else do you need to get started?

Communities need to agree on how to manage and govern their work, and may need help with community organizing and the facilitation of group decision-making. Agencies and programs need to involve their employees in creating a healthy workplace, one with open communications and mutual respect between management and staff. Both kinds of efforts need to support the growth and development of new and existing leaders. You can test your progress on implementing RBA with the self assessment questions in Appendix A.

Where can you get more information?

Consider reading the rest of this book. Go to the website raguide.org, which is an implementation guide for the RBA framework, sponsored by national, state and local foundations, including the Annie E. Casey Foundation, the Foundation Consortium for California's Children and Youth, the Colorado Foundation, the Nebraska Children and Families Foundation and the Finance Project. It contains answers to over 50 commonly asked questions and provides tools, formats, exercises, and links to other important resources.

Be a good consumer of advice. You shop carefully when you buy a car or refrigerator. You should also be a good consumer of advice. Learn about different approaches and pick the one that makes the most sense for you and your organization. Find out what other people's experience has been. Many frameworks look good on paper but are very difficult to implement and sustain. Consider using the criteria: Simple, Common Sense, Plain Language, Minimum Paper, and Useful, as a way to compare different approaches and make the best choice.

Be independent of consultants. Your organization needs to develop its own capacity to do this work, independent of consultants. There are many consulting firms out there willing to charge you a lot of money for things that you can and should do for yourself. No amount of consulting time and money can substitute for the will to change. Use consultants to get started if necessary, but train your own people to be in-house experts. Be careful about what you will have to pay for the rights to use a particular framework. Everything in this book is free for use by government and non-profit organizations.[13]

---

13. And small for-profit consulting firms. See the notices following Chapter 9 for details.

WHERE RESULTS-BASED ACCOUNTABILITY THINKING HAS WORKED

The thinking process at the heart of Results-Based Accountability is naturally found in many successful change efforts, and has been around in different forms for a long time. The sections between each chapter contain examples of where this thinking has worked, including examples at both the population and performance levels. In each case, a group of people started with an end condition of well-being and at least one measurement of that condition. They studied the causes behind this condition, the history of where they had been, and where they were headed if things didn't change. They engaged a diverse group of partners from their community. They looked at the successful work of others and considered their options about what works. They took action, not as a one-time effort, but as a continuous process. And they produced measurable improvement in the well-being of their communities and the performance of their programs. Three of the stories are examples of where people used RBA methods without calling it that (Mothers Against Drunk Driving, Tillamook and Boston). These are stories that helped shape the original development of RBA. The other four more recent stories in Vermont, North Lincolnshire, Montgomery County and Santa Cruz, show where people deliberately applied the methods in this book.

Mothers Against Drunk Driving[14]

Mothers Against Drunk Driving (MADD) provides one of the best examples of people who set out to measurably change a condition of well-being and succeeded. MADD was formed in California in 1980 by a group of women who got together after each had lost a member of their family to drunk driving. They were appalled at the growing number of deaths due to drunk driving and society's seeming tolerance of this tragedy. Figure 1.3 shows estimated and actual alcohol related traffic fatalities from 1975 to 2003.

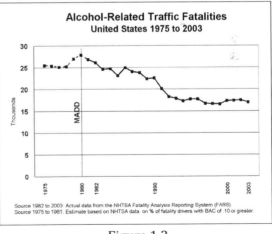

Figure 1.3

In 1980, no one had written the book on how to reduce alcohol related traffic fatalities. MADD had to invent one. Many of the actions that MADD has taken are familiar. These

---

14.   Source: Publications and statistical summaries from Mothers Against Drunk Driving, Irving, Texas (madd.org). Their assistance is gratefully acknowledged.

include direct actions such as Operation Prom / Graduation, where young people at the time of the Spring dance, sign a pledge not to drink and drive. Other strategies include the Red Ribbon campaign to raise public awareness about drunk driving, and the designated driver programs.

MADD has also supported federal, state and local legislative changes including age 21 drinking laws, license revocation for repeat offenders, victims' rights and victims' compensation laws. Compared to 1980, an estimated 9,000 lives are saved each year in addition to billions of dollars in direct and indirect damage to peoples' lives and property.[15] This number is even more dramatic when you consider that there are approximately 70 injuries for every death.[16] We still have a long way to go. In 2003, there were 17,000 alcohol related traffic fatalities in the US, approximately 47 every day.

The story of MADD's success includes all of the elements of the RBA change process. They started with a result: a society free of the devastating effects of drunk driving. They tracked an indicator of this result, the rate of alcohol-related traffic fatalities. They studied the story behind alcohol related fatalities. They engaged a diverse set of partners. They considered what could work and took action. And they were never satisfied with a finished action plan, but repeatedly updated and improved their work.

MADD doesn't claim full credit for these reductions. They recognize the contributions of many partners, including schools, courts, law enforcement, the media and state legislatures. They also recognize the contributions of improved car safety during this period. However, MADD's story teaches us not to wait for a federal grant, not to wait for the research community to give us the proven answer, and not to measure our success by how many projects we have implemented or how much money we raised, but by whether the curve has turned.

In spite of this success, there is a disturbing question that comes from looking at the data. After considerable progress in the 1980's and early 1990's, the baseline has remained essentially flat. Whatever we as a nation are doing is not working to make further progress. Somehow we have got to make the next increment of progress. A reinvigorated effort, using RBA methods to dig into causes, engage new partners and devise the next generation of strategies, could help to do that.

---

15.   The direct cost of alcohol related crashes was estimated at $44 billion in 1993. This estimate does not include pain, suffering and lost quality of life, which raise the alcohol-related crash figure to $134 billion.

16.   Statistical Abstract of the United States, 2003, Table 1058.

Chapter 2:

THE BUILDING BLOCKS OF
RESULTS-BASED ACCOUNTABILITY

Chapter 1 provided a summary of the entire Results-Based Accountability framework. In this chapter, we look at the conceptual building blocks of RBA. We first address the need for a common language by identifying four of the most important RBA ideas and the words used to label those ideas. We look at the differences between Population and Performance Accountability and why this distinction is so important. And we describe the RBA thinking process that is used in later chapters to get from talk to action for programs and communities.

Common language, Common sense and Common ground

Common language is not about English versus other languages. It's about the fundamental need we have to understand what people mean when they say something. There is currently an appalling lack of discipline in how we use language when we work together on community well-being and program performance. The usual state of affairs is a Tower of Babel where no one really understands what is being said, but everyone politely pretends that they do. You wouldn't get on an airplane or submit yourself to surgery if the pilots and surgeons routinely used jargon they didn't understand. It would be dangerous. The community and program work we do together is every bit as complicated as flying an airplane. But confusing jargon is the norm,[17] and this sometimes makes us dangerous. Words like "result," "indicator," and "performance measure" have many possible meanings. Unless we agree on the meaning of the words we use, it is impossible to make progress. So, we will spend some time developing a common language.

Common sense is about the way the rest of the world works. Any successful human enterprise starts with ends and works backward to means. In business, the ends are profit, return on investment and growth in equity, and we have many sophisticated ways of measuring the success of companies.[18] But look at any successful enterprise: business, the military, the sports world, the faith community. They all work backward from ends to means. In fact, everyone does this except those of us in the public and non-profit sectors. We get so tied up in the means, the particular program, project or

---

[17]   In one city, the human services agency and its partners used a jumble of 67 words or word combinations with no clear definitions. They wondered why they weren't making progress.

[18]   Notwithstanding the dramatic failures of Enron, WorldCom and Wall Street, proving that the business world also requires a new infusion of accountability.

initiative, that we lose sight of the ends that we are trying to accomplish. RBA is built on the simple notion that in all of our work it is possible to articulate ends in plain English,[19] in terms that taxpayers and voters can understand, and use the ends as the starting point to work backwards to means, because it's just common sense.

Common ground is about the political nature of this work. Everything in this book, from the first word to the last, is political. This is not necessarily bad. Politics is how we make decisions in our society. Look at the political system at the national, state, and local levels, and you often see people fighting with each other. Most often they are fighting about means and not ends. There is remarkable agreement across our societies that teen pregnancy is bad for our young people. We fight about whether to hand out condoms or preach abstinence. This is a debate about means. The agreement about teen pregnancy is remarkably broadly based. When we articulate what we want in plain language, for example *Children Ready for School*, *Safe Communities* and *A Clean Environment*, it turns out that these kinds of statements are not Republican versus Democrat. They do not belong to the executive branch versus the legislative branch. They are not owned by a particular level of government. They represent a kind of common ground where people can come together and say, "Yes, those are the conditions we want here in our community, city, county, council, state, or nation." Now, let's see if we can have a healthy debate about the means to get there.

The language of accountability

The Jargon Construction Kit[20] shows the words that are most commonly used in work on Population and Performance Accountability. If you want to make yourself sound superior, pick three or four of these words at random and string them together.

- Urgent measurable strategic indicators
- Targeted priority incremental goals
- Core qualitative systemic results
- (Insert your own example here).

I guarantee if you combine words in this way you will get away with it because people will be too embarrassed to ask you what you mean. I have a rule about language:

Figure 2.1

19. With plain English, I also include plain Spanish, plain Vietnamese, plain Farsi and all the other 150 languages now spoken in our communities.

20. The Lewis Carroll Center for Language Disorders is a subsidiary of the Fiscal Policy Studies Institute.

If anyone uses three or more of these words in the same sentence, they don't know what they're talking about.

It is quite common to find two people in the same meeting using the same word, "outcome" for example, with two entirely different ideas of what that word means. They end up talking right past each other. Have you had this experience? Almost everyone has.

It is possible to use language in a clear and disciplined way. This requires that we agree on definitions that start with ideas and not words. Words are just labels for ideas, and the same idea can have many different labels. The language of RBA starts with the following four ideas.[21] The first word listed is the label used in this book, with some alternatives shown in parentheses.

Results, Indicators, and Performance Measures
in Amharic, Cambodian, Laotian, Somali
Spanish, Tigrigna and Vietnamese

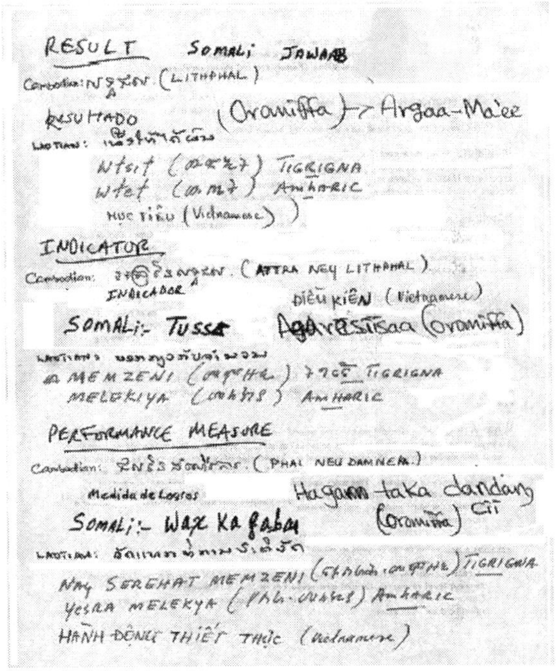

Thanks to the partners in White Center, Seattle for creating this picture.

Figure 2.2

A population **result** (or outcome or goal) is a condition of well-being for children, adults, families and communities, stated in plain language. Results are conditions that voters and taxpayers can understand. They are about the well-being of people in a community, city, county, state or nation. Results include: *Healthy Children, Children Ready for School, Children Succeeding in School, Strong Families, A Prosperous Economy, A Safe Community, A Clean Environment.*[22]

A population **indicator** (or benchmark[23]) is a measure that helps quantify the achievement of a result. Indicators answer the question: "How would we recognize this result

21. I presented the first version of these definitions in lectures in 1994 and published them in the paper "From Outcomes to Budgets" in June, 1995. These definitions and variations of the definitions are now widely used.
22. An interesting alternative definition of a result is offered by Con Hogan: "A condition of well-being for people in a place, stated as a complete sentence." This suggests the construction of a result as "All (people) in (place) are (condition)." e.g. "All babies in Vermont are born healthy."
23. In the business community, the word "benchmark" is not used in this way. It most often means an established standard or the level of performance of a successful competitor.

if we fell over it?" For example, the rate of low-birthweight babies helps quantify healthy births. Third grade reading scores help quantify whether children are succeeding in school today, and whether they were ready for school three years ago.[24] The crime rate helps quantify whether we are living in a safe community.

A **strategy** is a coherent set of actions that has a reasoned chance[25] of improving results. Strategies are made up of our best thinking about what works, and include the contributions of many partners. Strategies operate at both the population and performance levels.

A (program or service) **performance measure** (or performance indicator) is a measure of how well a program, agency or service system is working. The most important performance measures tell us whether program customers are better off. We refer to these measures as **customer** results to distinguish them from **population** results. RBA uses three types of performance measures: *How much did we do? How well did we do it? Is anyone better off?* The principal distinction in these definitions is between ends and means. Results and indicators are about the end conditions we want for children, adults, families and communities. Strategies and performance measures are about the means to get there.

Here's a quiz to see if you understand the distinction between results, indicators, strategies and performance measures. Notice how some of these statements sound alike, but in fact describe very different things. See the footnote for the answers.[26]

Figure 2.3

a. _____ Safe community

b. _____ Crime rate

c. _____ Average police department response time

d. _____ Installation of new street lights to make people feel safer

e. _____ Healthy people

f. _____ Rate of deaths from heart disease

---

24. In economics we have leading and lagging indicators. Percent reading at grade level in 3rd grade is a lagging indicator of school readiness 3 or 4 years earlier. Given the sad state of our data on young children, these lagging indicators are sometimes the best we have.
25. The "reasoned chance" part of strategies is sometimes called "theory of change."
26. a. result b. indicator c. performance measure d. strategy e. result f. indicator g. result h. indicator i. strategy j. performance measure

g. _____ People have living wage jobs and income

h. _____ Percent of people who have living wage jobs and income

i. _____ Recruit industries that pay living wages.

j. _____ Percent of participants in a job training program who get living wage jobs.

Being disciplined about language requires effort. We are fighting decades of sloppy practice and the clear use of language will not happen overnight. In the beginning, you may be the only one in your group who pays attention to language discipline. It takes some courage to help the group move in this direction. When someone uses a word like "result," ask them to give an example. The example will help you figure out which idea goes with the word they are using. If they say "The result I want is to live in a safe community," then you know they are using the word "result" to describe an end condition of well-being, as in the definition above. If they say, "The result I want is a new community center," then you know they are using the word "result" to describe a possible strategy. You can politely rephrase what they said. "What you mean is that we should build a community center as part of our strategy to make the neighborhood safe. A safe neighborhood is the result we want."

Tool for Choosing a Common Language
Schematic

Ideas	Possible Labels		Choice
	Words	Modifiers	
1. A condition of well-being for children, adults, families and communities	Result Outcome Goal	Population Community-wide	1._____
2.			2._____
3.			3._____
4.			4._____
5.			5._____
6.			6._____

FPSI

Figure 2.4

Rosetta Stone

Figure 2.5

Humor can lighten this process. We shouldn't embarrass people for "wrong" language usage. We don't need the language police. Groups will gradually learn that they can be more effective when people are clear about what they are trying to say and how they say it.

The Tool for Choosing a Common Language can help groups reach agreement about language. The full tool is provided in Appendix B and is shown as a schematic in Figure 2.4. The tool is set up in three columns. The first column is a list of the most important accountability ideas we need to keep straight. The next column shows choices about possible labels for these ideas. The last column is a place to record your choice. The only rule in completing this form is that you can only use a specific word or combination of words once in the last column.

If you sit down and fill out this form with a group of people, then you will have reached agreement on a common language. A few years ago, I worked with a group of state and local educators over a two day period and at the end of the second day they filled out the entire form in 20 minutes. They had been fighting with each other for 20 years about various things, but they filled out the form in 20 minutes because they realized that there was no chance of making progress unless they had a way to talk to each other.

If you cannot get people to agree on a common language, then try creating a translation guide or "Rosetta Stone." The Rosetta Stone, you may recall, was the tablet they found in the Nile Delta that finally allowed the translation of hieroglyphics. It showed the message in both hieroglyphic symbols and in Greek. You can create the equivalent of the Rosetta Stone by listing ideas down the left column of a chart. Then, in the columns to the right, list the words that different groups use to label each idea. This will allow you to translate the words that people use back to a central set of ideas. Over time, people may realize that this is an inefficient way to work and might be willing to move toward a using a common language. It is sometimes effective to have a small committee make recommendations about common language that the whole organization can then adopt.

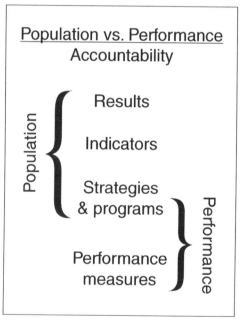

Figure 2.6

The difference between Population and Performance Accountability

We've been using the word "accountability" from the beginning. What is accountability? Accountability is a relationship between persons or groups, where one is responsible to another for something important.[27] The superintendent is accountable to the parents and school board for the success of the children in the school system. The teen pregnancy task force is accountable to the community for reducing the rate of teen pregnancy. Accountability means that it matters if we succeed or fail. It matters if things get better or worse.

As we noted in the first chapter, RBA has two components: Population Accountability and Performance Accountability. In Population Accountability, a group of partners

---

27. Like all the other words in this field, the word "accountability" sometimes carries a lot of baggage. If you don't like the word, then pick something else. Plain language is always best, so call RBA "The way we work together to make things better," or TWWWTTMTB or T4W3MB.

takes on responsibility for the well-being of a population in a geographic area. In Performance Accountability, a manager or group of managers takes responsibility for the performance of a program, agency or service system. These two kinds of accountability have been badly confused over the last 50 years or more.

Population Accountability is about a geographic area, e.g. all people in the world, all children in Australia, all elders in Philadelphia, whole populations without regard to whether they are getting service from anyone or not. This first kind of accountability is, by definition, bigger than any one department or program. It is bigger than government.

Performance Accountability is about our role as managers, and how well we run the programs for which we are responsible. Performance Accountability focuses on the well-being of customer populations, as distinct from whole populations. Performance Accountability operates at all levels of the organization from the smallest program up to the performance of the agency as a whole. And, it operates at the level of service systems, collections of agencies with related purposes and common customers.

Population and Performance Accountability together span the entire distance from the well-being of the world population to the performance of the smallest programs in the government and non-government sectors and everything in between. This makes RBA one of the most comprehensive of all frameworks.

Let's revisit the MASH example we used earlier to illustrate the difference between Population and Performance Accountability. The MASH units were processing casualties from the Korean War. Child protection units in our states, counties and cities are processing the casualties from the wars that go on in families. MASH units and child protection units are both service providers with a distinct service population. In each case, it is possible to develop performance measures for these operations and hold the managers accountable for the performance of their program or agency.

No one expected the MASH units to end the Korean War. Progress at this level required the work of many different players, far beyond the contribution of the MASH unit. In the same way, no one should expect child protection, by itself, to end child abuse. Progress on reducing child abuse in a city, county, state or nation will require a wide range of partners beyond child protection services.

The principle distinction here has to do with <u>who</u> is responsible. With programs and agencies, we can identify the manager or managers who should be held responsible. For cross community conditions such as *Safe Children* or *Clean Environment*, there is no one person or agency that can be held responsible. Population Accountability requires broad partnerships that take **collective** responsibility for progress.

This means that all program and agency managers, have two kinds of responsibility. They have a **program management responsibility** to produce the best possible performance for the services they administer. And they have a **community leadership responsibility** to bring together the necessary partners to make progress at the population level.

If success at the population level depends on partnerships, then it is unfair to hold any single agency responsible for community conditions. Managers put in this position will be rightly fearful of criticism about conditions that they cannot possibly remedy by themselves. This kind of unfair responsibility causes managers to be defensive, closed and narrowly protective of their agencies, precisely the kind of behavior that works against any chance for real progress.

Let's look at a few quick examples of the difference between Population and Performance Accountability.

EXAMPLES OF POPULATION ACCOUNTABILITY
(Community, City, County, State, Nation and World)

Population: Entire world population
Population result: World peace
Indicators: Number of current wars, percent of world population living in poverty.

Population: All residents of Pennsylvania
Population result: Clean Environment
Indicators: Percent of days below air quality standards, percent of contaminated stream-miles.

Population: All residents of Philadelphia
Population result: Safe Community
Indicators: Violent crime rate, percent of residents who feel safe.

Figure 2.7

EXAMPLES OF PERFORMANCE ACCOUNTABILITY
(Program, Agency and Service System)

Program: The Peace Corps
Performance Measures: Percent of countries accepting / requesting volunteers, percent of volunteers who complete the program, percent of volunteers who extend their service.

Program: Pennsylvania Department of Environmental Protection
Performance Measure: Percent of cited industries that fully implement clean up orders.

Program: Philadelphia Police Department
Performance Measure: Average response time, percent of crimes with successful prosecution.

Figure 2.8

These are examples where the population / performance distinction is most clear. No program, no agency, no government alone can produce *World Peace, Safe Communities or A Clean Environment*. We can, however, expect the managers of the Peace Corps, the Department of Environmental Protection and the Police Department to demonstrate high quality performance on the measures for their programs. And we can expect them to participate in larger efforts to promote improved conditions in their communities.

For each program there is one or more population results to which the program directly contributes. Each program needs to understand and report on these conditions, in addition to reporting on their own performance. The police department should report on the safety of the community (crime rates) while at the same time reporting on its performance (response time). These two types of reporting should be clearly separated, so that legislatures, county commissioners and city councils can see clearly the population conditions for which the program manager **shares** responsibility, and the performance conditions for which the program manager **owns** responsibility.

Another little understood characteristic of the relationship between Population and Performance Accountability is its "non-linear" nature. This means that there is not a clean one-to-one correspondence between programs and population results. This can be illustrated by the odd convention adopted in one state budget where each program of state government was assigned a unique four digit number that precisely placed the program within the state government organizational structure (no problem here), and then assigned it to a single population result (problem). So the division of water quality fit cleanly inside the Department of Environmental Quality. And the Department of Environmental Quality was then assigned to one population result: *Clean Environment*.

This practice of assigning an agency to one result derives from the accounting practice of rolling up smaller accounts into larger accounts. The accounting paradigm works fine inside the bureaucracy. Programs roll up to divisions and divisions roll up to departments. But the roll-up relationship breaks down once we cross the line from Performance to Population Accountability. There is no question that the Department of Environment contributes to *A Clean Environment*. But it also contributes to many other population results as well, including *Healthy People, Economic Prosperity*, and *Safe Communities*. Assigning programs and agencies to a single population result obscures these other important relationships. It makes it appear that the Department of Environment is solely responsible for *A Clean Environment*. So when the Economic Development task force invites the Department of Environment to partner with them, Environment feels entitled to say "Sorry, we are responsible for *A Clean Environment* not *Economic Prosperity*. Working on your department's result is not our job." RBA makes clear that each agency contributes to many results and the need for broad partnerships becomes obvious.

A number of other conceptual models, notably those with roots in the logic model literature, tend to reinforce the flawed view of a linear relationship between Performance and Population Accountability. These models do not sharply distinguish between the two. Instead they often present a smooth continuum from inputs to outputs to outcomes to community results (or goals as they are most often called in these models). There is nothing to suggest that crossing over from performance to population conditions is anything more than the next step in this linear progression. The models tend to encourage managers to think that they have some form of prime responsibility for at least one community condition that their program aims to "impact." This way of thinking is counterproductive. It heightens fear in managers and takes energy away from their efforts to improve performance.

The primary thinking process in the RBA framework works in the opposite direction from logic models, from community results backward to programs. In this direction, the non-linear relationship is obvious. If we want to measurably improve water quality, then we must consider the many partners with a role to play in such improvement and what contribution each might make.

Government departments often make the mistake of claiming one or more population conditions as "departmental results." So, for example, the health department claims *Healthy People* as its own result; the department of environment claims *Clean Environment* as its own and so forth. The old "mission, vision, values, goals, objectives" thinking makes this appear quite reasonable. "Our mission is to improve the health of all residents of our county. And here's how we propose to do that." It works fine until the department finds itself out on a limb being criticized for why population health is not improving. If the department decides to introduce the idea of shared accountability at this point, it looks like the department is being defensive and making excuses for its poor performance. It is far better to set up the notion of shared accountability for population results from the very beginning.

Population and Performance Accountability are two different creatures with an unusual non-linear relationship.[28] As we shall see in a later chapter, the boundary between these two kinds of accountability is itself quite complex (and governed by chaos and complexity theory), but for now let's leave the distinction in its simplest form.

If you've read the book straight through to this point, it's time to take a break. While you're getting your snack, try this mental exercise. Think about one program that you've worked with in the past. Think of the population results to which that program contributed. Think of all the partners outside the program that had a role to play in improving those results. See if separating the performance and population components of your work relieves some stress about unfair responsibility, allows a clearer focus on performance for customers, and stimulates new ideas about how to collaborate with others.

[28.] See also "creature non-linear relationship counseling."

The Results-Based Accountability thinking process[29]

The idea of using results to make decisions is not new. The world has always been about results. The notion that ends drive means is the foundation of everything from evolutionary survival to business profits. Some of the earliest results systems are shown in Figure 2.9, along with some of the earliest indicators. Our species has survived so far because we are motivated to reproduce and find food. In each case, a picture of success motivates action.

RBA makes use of this ancient thinking process. The ends in RBA are arguably the most important, namely the conditions of well-being of people and communities. Let's start with something simpler than the survival of humanity. Let's start with a leaking roof.

The leaking roof thinking process

Consider the following Socratic dialogue from Plato's famous tract on roof repair:

Socrates: Have you ever had a leaking roof?

Student: *Yes!*

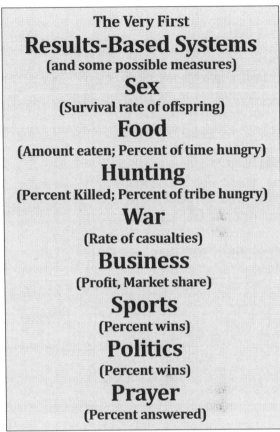

The Very First
Results-Based Systems
(and some possible measures)
Sex
(Survival rate of offspring)
Food
(Amount eaten; Percent of time hungry)
Hunting
(Percent Killed; Percent of tribe hungry)
War
(Rate of casualties)
Business
(Profit, Market share)
Sports
(Percent wins)
Politics
(Percent wins)
Prayer
(Percent answered)

Figure 2.9

How can you tell that it's leaking?

It's dripping on my head. It's coming down the walls. There's water on the floor.

So you **experience** *a leaking roof in these different kinds of ways.*

Yes.

Now, if you wanted to **measure** *how badly it was leaking, what could you do?*

I could put out a bucket and measure the number of inches in the bucket after each rainstorm!

[29.] Well, it took long enough to get here!

Yes, very good. And that's the graph in Figure 2.10. The three points represent the number of inches of water in the bucket from the last three rainstorms.

Where do you think this line is headed if we don't do something about the roof?

It will keep going up.

Right. The roof is not going to fix itself. We can predict that the inches of water in the bucket will increase. This is what we mean by a **baseline**. A baseline has two parts, an historical part that tells us where we've been (the last three rainstorms), and a forecast part that shows where we're heading if we don't do something different.

If you're living in this place, it is **not OK** for the leak to get worse. You want to follow a path to zero inches of water just as fast as possible. This is what we mean by **turning the curve** or beating the baseline. Now, what's the first thing you do when you have a leaking roof?

Look for the cause of the leak.

Right. Someone has to get up on the roof and figure out why it's leaking. This is the **story behind the baseline.**

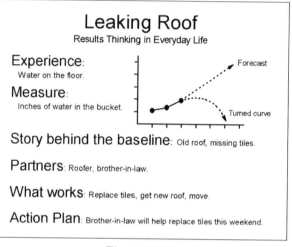

Figure 2.10

Who are some potential **partners** who might help you fix the leak?

A roofer, a family member, a money lender...

Now **what works** to actually fix a leak? What are some of your choices here?

I could patch it.

And there are some choices about patching materials, right?

Tar, shingles...

Duct tape.

Or I could get a whole new roof. Maybe I need to sell the house and move to a drier climate.

So let's review. You've got a leaking roof. It's getting worse and will keep getting worse unless you do something about it. You've got some potential partners and some ideas about how the roof might be fixed.

Now, here's the important final question. What are you actually going to do?

I haven't decided yet.

OK. But whatever you finally decide to do becomes your **action plan**. You decide you can't afford to move or replace the whole roof. Your brother-in-law will come over this weekend and together you will patch the roof as best you can.

You don't know my brother-in-law!

So you implement your action plan, and now what do you do?

I'd wait for the next rainstorm, or spray a hose on the roof, to see if it's still leaking.

What happens if there is still water in the bucket after the next rainstorm or the hose test? Is the roof fixed?

No.

So what do you do now?

I guess I'd have to start over again.

That's right. You missed the cause of the leak the first time. Or maybe there were two leaks and you only found one. Someone has to get back up there and find out why it's really leaking. You think about partners again. Your brother-in-law doesn't seem to know anything about fixing roofs.

I told you.

You would think about what works again. Maybe duct tape wasn't the best choice of patching material.

It was your idea.

And you would create a second action plan and implement it. Then what do you do?

Wait for the next rainstorm.

*Right. This is an **iterative** (or repetitive) **process** until there is no more water in the bucket.

This is the common sense thinking process behind RBA! It's how we solve problems in our everyday lives. Communities working to improve their quality of life or managers working to improve their program's performance can use this same process. If you understand this process, you can skip the next dialogue and go do something more fun.

Thanks, Socrates. See you around.

In chapters 3 and 4, we will apply this thinking process to things that are far more complicated than a leaking roof. We will look at the well-being of our children and the performance of important programs and agencies. But it will be the same process.

Now, consider this. **You could have zero inches of water in the bucket and the roof is still not fixed.** Perhaps the water is coming down the inside of one of the walls, and you don't know this until three months later when the wall caves in. The purpose of the work is not actually zero inches of water in the bucket. It's a fixed roof. We use inches of water in the bucket to represent or approximate this condition. That's the nature of data. It is a tool to approximate the conditions we are trying to create. We must be careful that we don't put data on a pedestal and make it the purpose of the work. Data is never the purpose of the work.

Notice that we quickly identified the "inches of water in the bucket" measure. With a leaking roof, it's pretty obvious what's important and what could be measured. However, with communities or programs, the choice of what to measure is much more complicated. We will address the process of choosing indicators and performance measures in the next two chapters. Notice that when we are fixing a leaking roof, we don't actually put out a bucket and measure the inches of water. We don't create a graph. We judge success entirely on the basis of experience. When we stop seeing water, we consider the roof fixed. It is also possible to do this for community results or program performance. We can judge whether our children are safe, or our program is working, based on impressions, anecdotes and stories. But when we consider these more important conditions without using data, we really don't know if things are getting better or worse. When we raise the stakes from a leaking roof to the quality of life of our children or the performance of our programs, data becomes much more important.

Finally, the RBA thinking process is not necessarily linear. The steps in this process can be done in almost any order, as long as you do them all. Finding a partner to help is often the first thing to do. There is one place, however, where the sequence of thought is very important. Thinking about causes should always precede thinking about solutions. This is the common sense diagnostic process used in medicine. Doctors diagnose the illness before they prescribe treatment. In RBA, the story behind the baseline should always precede thinking about actions.

Charts on the wall

If you ever get to London, take some time to visit the Churchill War Rooms. It's a fascinating place, an underground warren of little rooms across from St. James's Park where

Churchill and his generals ran their part of World War II. One of the rooms is the Map Room, and it's set up exactly like it was on the last day of the war. This was the place where everyone could see visually whether progress was being made on the various fronts of the war. If you're running an important enterprise, whether it is a community effort to reduce crime or an important program, you need to have the equivalent of a map room. The maps that go on the walls are the most important curves you are trying to turn.

This concept is all around you. If you're running a fund raising campaign, the chart on the wall is the amount collected against the goal, perhaps in the familiar United Way thermometer format. If you're running a business, the chart on the wall is profit, stock price or market share. If you're running a political campaign, the chart on the wall is fund raising and polling data.

What chart should you have on your wall? The population and performance sections of this book will help you decide what measures are most important. Then you should develop the baselines for these measures, print the charts on large paper and have them on the wall every time you meet with your partners. When people are distracted or in conflict, these charts can help bring people back to their common purposes. You can also put a chart or two outside your office door, declaring to the world (or at least your colleagues, or maybe just yourself) the results that you think are most important and the curves you are trying to turn. It is a reminder of purpose each time you come and go that will stimulate interesting discussions.

In Vermont, the Agency for Human Services, the Department of Education and their local partners created 10 charts, one for each of the 10 Vermont outcomes. The charts show the baseline data for the indicators associated with each outcome. These charts were posted on a wall in the meeting room where the state and local partners met each month. In Portsmouth, UK, the Department of Social Services designated a place near the water cooler on the top floor where the agency's most important performance measures were shown. In the Maryland Leadership in Action Program, participants start each meeting with a "data walk" where people walk in pairs down a row of charts showing whether children in Maryland are ready for school.

Of all the things you can do with the ideas in this book, putting a baseline chart on the wall may be the simplest and easiest step you can take. Imagine how impressed your visitors will be when they walk into your meeting room or office and see data on the wall!

The false gods

Once you understand that results are the true ends of our work, it becomes clear that some of the other things we have been working on for all these years are means, and not ends in themselves. These are the false gods.

Collaboration: We have created a service system for children and families where it is entirely possible for public health, mental health, juvenile justice, social services, and the schools to all be working with the same family and not even know it. We must find a way to make sense out of this crazy system, and collaboration between partners is an important part of the answer.

But collaboration has come to be seen as an end in itself. I go to some communities and ask "What have you folks been doing for children and families?" And they answer, "We have a collaborative!" The collaborative has become the purpose of the work.

The collaborative should never be the purpose of the work. The collaborative is a means to bring people together to take action. In the past decade, we have seen a proliferation in the number of collaboratives. You can go to some communities and see that dozens have been created. (One county published a directory of collaboratives over 50 pages long). Recently, the Centers for Disease Control (CDC) in Atlanta announced that they are tracking a new mortality category, "death by collaboration." When you look at the membership of all these groups, it's the same people, going from meeting to meeting. Eventually they expire and we've got to replace them. We now have a way to count their deaths.

We need a period of mergers and acquisitions, to return to the original idea of having one, two, or at best a handful of places where this work is brought together. That will require that local people rise up in rebellion. Every time the federal government, state government or a foundation makes a grant, they require that a collaborative advisory body be set up for that particular grant. Collaboratives quickly develop a life of their own, and then work to maintain their existence. It requires considerable vision and courage to admit that a particular group no longer needs a separate identity. Grantees have to say back to the funders, "We will not set up a new collaborative. We'll use an existing one."

Systems Reform and Service Integration: The best work on systems reform and service integration is about a very simple idea. Some day we would like to have a service system that has a **front room and a back room.** In the front room, children and families will get what they **need** based on what they need, not all the crazy categories we have created over the last 50 years. In the back room, we'll categorize people as much as possible so that we can claim every conceivable dollar to pay for what's in the front room. Right now, all we have is the back room. The question, "What do you need?" becomes "What can we pay for?" The funding system largely drives the service system. One day we'll have a service system with a front room and back room and systems reform and service integration will help get us there.

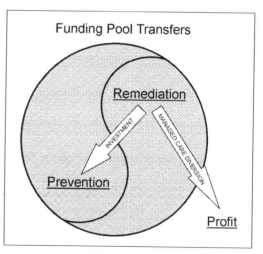

Figure 2.11

Funding Pools and Fund Flexibility: In the United States, the current service system for children and families is a 50 year accumulation of political deal-making rather than any sensible way to serve people. It is a highly categorical system that is so restrictive that we sometimes think the only way to fund innovative service is to create innovative financing methods. Hence, the funding pool idea. There is nothing wrong with innovative financing, but funding pools and fund flexibility schemes are sometimes seen as a panacea. "If only we had a fund pool, all would be right with the world." The problem is that funding pools are very difficult to create and are usually completely useless. Partner agencies take money that is already discretionary and put it into a funding pool where it is still discretionary. We simply move the location of the fight about how to use this money from one place to another.

If you want to see a funding pool that is useful, look at the Iowa Decategorization Program, or "Decat" for short.[30] They combined money from the most intensive treatment end of the system, including out-of-home foster care, juvenile justice and mental health, with the money designed to keep families safely together, including family preservation, family support and respite care. The state of Iowa gives the local Decat boards considerable flexibility in how the money is spent. If the Decat boards can save money on the deep end of the system, while keeping children safe, they can keep those savings, transfer them over and buy more preventive services. This mechanism is grounded in a very simple two page piece of legislation[31] that allows Iowa state General Funds to be rolled across fiscal years. It is the only such instance I know of in the country. Even though Decat is called a funding pool, no money is actually physically pooled. The money all remains in separate accounts. This avoids the accounting and control difficulties that go with putting different fund sources in a single account. But those separate accounts are managed **as if** they were pooled. The idea of a "virtual funding pool" is another important Iowa innovation that is not often recognized.

Useful funding pools like Iowa's have the characteristic of combining remediation dollars with prevention dollars. When the two are combined, it creates a natural incentive to save on remediation expenses so that you can spend more on prevention, an incentive that does not exist with 100% discretionary fund pools. This packaging of remediation and prevention dollars is the idea behind medical managed care. Unfortunately, in managed care, this good idea has gone astray because the transfer from remediation to prevention is undermined by the transfer to profit.[32]

---

30.   Bill Rust, "Decat in the Hat: Iowa's Successful First Step Toward Devolving Resources, Responsibility, And Accountability For Child And Family Outcomes," Advocasey, aecf.org/publications/advocasey/decat/building.

31.   Passed in 1987 with the leadership of Charles Bruner and Doug Nelson.

32.   Managed care contracts should have graduated profit caps (e.g. managed care contractors keep 100% of the first 1% of profits, 50% of the 2nd percent and so forth) so that some of the remediation to prevention transfer incentive is preserved.

Reorganization: If a bureaucracy does not work, it is not the fault of its organization. It's the fault of its leadership. I worked for state government for 19 years, and we had a reorganization every year. No kidding. Some were big. Some were small. None produced anything but a lot of paperwork and anxiety. I have come to believe that reorganizations are almost always a waste of time. They are used to give the appearance of action when leaders don't know what else to do. Reorganizations take two years out of the life any organization while people try to figure out their new jobs and how they fit into the new arrangement. There is almost nothing that needs to be done, that can't be done with the existing organization **if there is the will to do it**. There are many other ways to shake up an organization and improve performance. The best way is to set performance expectations, use measures and track performance, as recommended in this very book.

There are two reorganization pendulums that swing back and forth and drive cycles of one reorganization after another. This is the closest that scientists have come to identifying a perpetual motion machine:

The change between centralized and decentralized structures: Move all functions to the central office. Two years later decentralize all functions back to the regional offices.

The change between combined organizations and separate organizations: Put all children and family services in one department. Two years later, put all services back in the departments from which they came.

These movements happen within departments and across departments, and provide endless opportunities to rationalize inaction by changing structure. If you, as a manager or leader, really want people to work together differently, then **direct them to work differently under the current organizational structure.** If it actually works better then, and only then, codify it with a formal change in the organization.

The false gods are distractions. Collaboration, system reform, fund flexibility and reorganization have value only when they support the end conditions we hope to create, the improved performance of our programs and improved conditions of well-being for children, adults, families and communities.

Passion and Discipline
Figure 2.12

Turn the curve tables: passion and discipline

I learned an important lesson about RBA by making a mistake one day. I was working with partnership groups from across Vermont, and at the end of a long and tiring day I said to the Brattleboro team, "Stop talking. Just pick a curve and turn it." They went back to Brattleboro and spent much of the next several months debating which curve to pick and that was pretty much my fault. I returned to meet with the Brattleboro partnership. Out of that meeting came an idea, first put forward by one of their partners, Tom Redden. Maybe the role of the partnership is not to pick the one and only thing the community is going to work on. Maybe the partnership's role is to set tables. These "Turn the Curve" tables could be set by result (children ready for school or safe community) or by indicator (teen pregnancy rate or air quality rate). People would come to these tables because they are passionate about turning these curves.

I believe that there are two ingredients necessary to make this work successful, passion and discipline. Passion without discipline won't accomplish much. Discipline by itself can actually be dangerous. Put passion and discipline together and you can accomplish almost anything.

If you create a Turn the Curve table in your community and bring passion to the table, RBA can be the discipline. The success stories between chapters show all the major elements of the RBA process. Each group of people started with an easily understood result. Each had one or more curves to turn. Each group studied the story behind the curves. Each brought together a diverse group of partners. The partners learned as much as they could about what works. And they took action, and improved their action plans over time. I developed RBA in part from observing and analyzing these kind of successful efforts and trying to figure out the thread of thinking that got people successfully from talk to action. RBA thinking is the discipline that made these passionate people successful.

WHERE RESULTS-BASED ACCOUNTABILITY
THINKING HAS WORKED

Tillamook County, Oregon[33]

Tillamook is a small county on the northwest coast of Oregon. It is famous for its cheese and other dairy products. People there like to say they have more cows than people. Back in the early 1990's, the state of Oregon issued a report card comparing the 36 counties in Oregon on their teen pregnancy rates. Tillamook came out worse than all but two counties. It came as a shock to the people who lived there. They didn't realize that they had a problem with teen pregnancy, certainly not that bad compared to their neighbors.

A few years before the report card came out, there had been a proposal on the table to build health clinics in Tillamook County's high schools. Tillamook is a very conservative county, both politically and socially, and most residents didn't want health clinics in their high schools. They didn't think it was any business of the schools to provide health services.[34]

When the teen pregnancy report card came out, the question became, "If we're not going to have health clinics in our high schools, what <u>are</u> we going to do

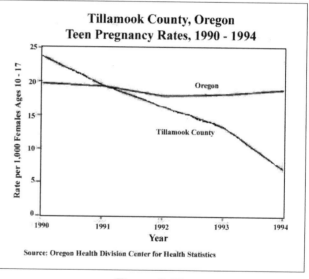

Figure 2.13

about our problem with teen pregnancy?" One by one, different people and groups came forward to be part of a community-wide effort. The strategy was simple: Get everyone - churches, public and private agencies, schools, health workers and families - to acknowledge the problem and commit themselves to doing what they could to change it. The controversial nature of the problem was turned into an asset. The widely different views of leaders helped motivate different sectors of the community to get involved. Here is a summary of some of the partners' actions:

---

[33]   Thanks to Sue Cameron and all the partners in Tillamook County.
[34]   We could no doubt debate this.

- Schools added self-esteem and sexuality education to their curriculum.
- Churches worked to open communication channels with teens, taught refusal skills, promoted abstinence, and provided recreation.[35]
- The county health department, with support from the county commissioners, expanded clinic hours and changed policy to assure that any teen who called the health department for information or services would be seen within 48 hours, not the two to three weeks previous practice.
- The YMCA sponsored a "teens at risk" program, providing recreation activities that kept teens busy and built self esteem.
- The community college worked with teens through the Tillamook Teen Parent Program to prevent second unintended pregnancies.
- The Commission on Children and Families funded a teen pregnancy prevention curriculum in the schools as well as counseling and support groups.
- The Tillamook County General Hospital and other partners, opened "Healthy Families of Tillamook County," a home-visiting and parenting program for all newborns.
- Other partners that made contributions included the Women's Crisis Center, the Tillamook Family Counseling Center, the Tillamook Bay Child Care Center, the Tillamook Bay Community College, and others.

In 1990 the teen pregnancy rate in Tillamook County was 24 per 1,000 girls ages 10 - 17.

Between 1990 and 1994, the teen pregnancy rate decreased to 7.1 per 1,000, the best rate in the state. The teen pregnancy rate for Oregon as a whole remained essentially flat during this period. The partners in Tillamook County do not attribute this success to any particular service, but rather to the combined effects of all the community partners.

The rebound effect: After 1994, the teen pregnancy rate rebounded, rising over the next five years almost back to where it had been in 1990. This rebound effect is quite common in community change processes. "We solved the problem of teen pregnancy! Thank God, we'll never have to worry about that again!" And so the partners shifted their focus, leadership changed, and the numbers went back up.

This loss of progress takes nothing away from the remarkable initial effort. However, it makes clear that part of the work with RBA is to expect the rebound and to build the community capacity necessary to sustain progress. There is not much value in a series of lapsed successes. How can communities sustain attention through changes of

---

35. Recreation services are among the most important things we do for young people. And recreation is so cheap compared to other services. Recreation services in many cities and counties have been cut back dramatically. The short paper, "The Most Results for the Least Money: A Recreation Entitlement," on resultsaccountability.com/publications, proposes creation of a recreation entitlement for all youth 7 to 17. Benefits would be widespread throughout the education, juvenile justice and other systems. Costs would be less that 2% of a typical city budget.

leadership and political priorities? There is not a simple answer to this question. However, recognizing the inevitability of a rebound without continued effort is a start.

There are two structural approaches that can help prevent a rebound. The first is the development of a regular report card on child and family well-being or community quality of life. Such report cards keep a spot light on the most important results and indicators, even the ones where we have made progress. This allows communities to see which indicators are at risk of rebound and work to maintain progress or at least stop the rebound before it takes too deep a hold. The second structure builds on the idea of "Turn the Curve Tables." For every condition, there are people in the community who continue to be passionate about the work, even after the political spotlight has turned elsewhere. By creating an on-going structure for people to meet, assess progress, and take action, the chances of a rebound can be reduced.

Chapter 3:

POPULATION ACCOUNTABILITY
for the well-being of whole populations in a community, city, county, state or nation

In this chapter, we address how partners can work together to improve quality of life for people in any geographic area, from communities to cities, counties, states and nations.

Getting from talk to action

Let's start by taking a quick spin through the steps of the Population Accountability process. Then we'll go back and look at some of the key concepts in more detail. The full thinking process is shown as a schematic (Figure 3.2) and in the form of 7 common sense questions (Figure 3.3).

Population: The Population Accountability process starts, as you might imagine, with identifying a population. Populations can be any whole population or subpopulation in a geographic area. The geographic area can be anything from the entire world to a nation, state, region, county, city or neighborhood. Within these geographic areas, the population can vary from all residents to any identifiable subpopulation. So we might talk about all residents of California, all elders in Miami, all overweight people in South Beach. The only populations not addressed are service populations, actual recipients of a particular service, which is the subject of Performance Accountability in the next chapter.[36]

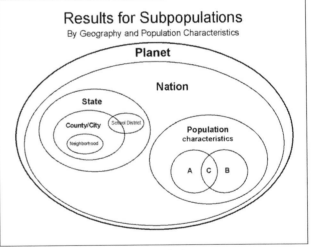

Figure 3.1

Results: Next, we ask what results (conditions of well-being stated in plain language) do we want for this population? In the leaking roof example, the implied result was "a non-

---

36. Note that the well-being of target populations, the intended group from which customers are drawn, is part of population and not Performance Accountability. The percent of the target population that actually receives service, or the percent of need met, is an important *How well did we do it?* measure. See Chapter 4.

leaking" roof. The California law that created the state's First 5 commissions[37] included the result that *Children Enter School Healthy and Ready to* Learn. Many states, counties, cities and communities have established a more complete set of results, addressing such conditions as *Children Born Healthy, Children Succeed in School, Safe Communities, A Prosperous Economy, A Clean Environment, All Residents Live in Safe, Stable and Affordable Housing.* The process can start with one result or many results. The only requirement is that results must be stated in plain language and not be about a program or about data.

Experience: How do we experience the results we want? How do we see, hear or feel them? If we are concerned about children being safe, for example, we might experience this by talking to our children at breakfast about whether they feel safe going to and coming from school, or whether they are worried about bullying We might observe if kids are wearing bike helmets as they ride around the neighborhood. (Research shows that failure to wear a bike helmet is the single leading cause of serious head injuries for children.) When Jerry Brown was running to be mayor of Oakland, California he said that he would know his neighborhood was safe when he could walk around without seeing so many iron grates on the windows. These are experiential versions of safety. There is no government report on iron grates.

Experience is the bridge between results and indicators.[38] It grounds the work in our daily lives. Each experience is a pointer to a potential indicator. If we experience *People in Safe, Stable, Affordable Housing* by seeing neighbors who own their own homes, then we can count the percent of people who own their own homes. **Experience can also be a temporary substitute for data** when there is no data. We can develop action plans designed to improve how we experience these conditions, while we work to create data that will help us track our progress.

Indicators: If we can identify results in plain language and in experiential terms, then we can look for data that tell us if we're getting these results or not. We are looking for 3 to 5 indicators for each result. The section below on Choosing Indicators presents a step by step method for doing this.

Data Development Agenda: An important by-product of selecting indicators is the creation of a Data Development Agenda, a prioritized list of where we need new or improved data. We never have all the data that we need, and we must continually work to get better data. Getting good data becomes more difficult as we move to progressively smaller geographic areas. National and state data is easiest to get. Neighborhood data is hardest.

Baselines: For each indicator we must create a baseline. Baselines have two parts: an historical part that tells where we have been and a forecast part that says where we are headed

---

37.   In 1998, California voters approved Proposition 10 to tax tobacco products and use the proceeds for services for children ages 0 - 5. The California law created a state First 5 Commission, and First 5 commissions for each of California's 58 counties.

38.   Thanks to Jolie Bain Pillsbury for helping me understand the importance of using experience as a bridge from results to indicators.

if we don't do anything more of different from what we are doing now. Baselines allow us to define success as turning the curve away from the baseline or beating the baseline.

Story behind the baselines: What is the story behind the baselines? If juvenile crime is rising in our community, why? If water quality is declining, why? What are the causes and forces at work behind these conditions? In public health they call this step epidemiology. Epidemiologists seek to understand the causes of a disease as pointers to actions that could reduce the incidence and prevalence of that disease. Similarly, if we understand what is causing crime or poor water quality, this will help us decide what actions to take that will best address these causes. Many processes skip this step and go directly to talking about actions. This is like a doctor prescribing medicine before diagnosing the what is wrong with you. In medicine, the proper sequence is diagnosis before treatment. In RBA, it's causes before action.

The word "story" is deliberately chosen here. Telling stories is the oldest form of communication, the oldest form of retained knowledge, and the oldest way in which we transform life experience into useful lessons. The idea of telling stories allows each partner to explain her or his perspective on how we got where we are today. This is the place to take stock of both positive and negative forces, what is working and what is not working. It is common to find many different opinions about causes. But it is not necessary for partners to reach agreement on a single story. Diverse points of view are assets to be respected, not obstacles to be overcome.

Many processes come to a dead halt because they require that all the partners agree with each other before going on to the next step. In RBA, diversity of opinion is the sign of a healthy process. You want as much information as you can get about causes, so that you have lots of choices about actions. For example, when working to reduce teen pregnancy, people from the faith community might argue that teen pregnancy is caused by moral decay. While public health folks might argue that it is caused by lack of access to reproductive health services. This is OK, because when it comes to action, the faith community can preach abstinence and the public health people can hand out condoms. Constructive diversity of opinions about causes leads to a richer action plan with a greater chance of success.

Information and research agenda about causes: Trying to understand the story behind current conditions will generate a need for more information. An Information and Research Agenda is a disciplined way of pursuing unanswered questions about causes. That agenda can guide information gathering between meetings, and, if resources are available, the actual commissioning of research. We often make incorrect assumptions about causes. For example, a study in Santa Cruz California challenged the view of homeless people as mostly single male alcoholics, and showed the high percent of evicted and displaced families with children.[39] Research can force us to ques-

---

39. Applied Survey Research, "Santa Cruz County Homeless 2000: Census and Needs Assessment, 2000," appliedsurveyresearch.org.

tion our biases. Research organizations, including local colleges and universities, have a very important role to play in doing this work.

This is also where **needs assessment** fits in. Many frameworks place needs assessment at the beginning of the process. But needs-based decision making processes tend to get mired in the simple fact that we can never meet all the needs. Incrementally meeting a greater percent of need misses the point. We meet needs for a reason and that reason is the improved well-being of children, adults, families and communities. Results and indicators should come first. Needs assessment comes later as a tool to help understand causes and craft solutions. Even in this role, needs assessment has limitations. Needs assessments predictably come to the conclusion that the problem is lack of services and the solution is more services. RBA instead challenges people to think more deeply about causes and to consider both service and non-service solutions that will make a difference.

Partners: Who are the partners who have a role to play in doing better? As we discussed earlier, no one program or agency can do it alone. The work requires contributions from a wide array of partners, public and private, across the community. In most processes, thinking about and assembling partners is one of the first steps taken, not something here in the middle. (See "Bringing people together to do this work," in Chapter 7). However, the work of adding partners is never finished. At each pass through the decision process, it is important to consider who is still needed at the table. The action plan should always have a component that addresses the recruitment and engagement of new partners. Remember that in practice, you never have everyone at the table. Processes that can't do anything until everyone is at the table typically don't do anything. **Inclusion is a process not an end point.** One of the tricks used in the Turn the Curve exercises in Appendix E is to ask participants to wear "two hats." In considering both the story and what works, participants are asked to represent both their own point of view and also the viewpoint of a partner not otherwise represented at the table. This enriches the discussion, and also makes the work more fun. It is important to press for consideration of non-traditional partners. When working on children succeeding in school, consider the children themselves as partners, and partners outside the education system, like the business community, media or the children's extended family. When working on healthy children, consider partners outside the health system. Think as broadly as possible and consider potential partners based on what they have to contribute, not on the likelihood of getting their contribution. A good set of results and a solid action plan will be a magnet for people and resources. One small neighborhood family support center in Baltimore City listed over 300 people and organizations on its partner list.

Don't forget about fiscal people. Fiscal partners are often left out of the discussions until the very end of the process, when they are then asked to help finance the efforts chosen by the group. At this point it is often difficult to get their cooperation. It is better for you, and for them, for fiscal partners to be involved early on.

What works: We now come to the central question: "What works to do better?" There are two natural pointers to answer this question. First, each part of the story behind the curve points to an action. If we know that one of the causes of teen pregnancy is that kids don't have anything to do after school, then this is a pointer to supervised recreation. If one of the reasons for increased fear of crime is poor lighting in the neighborhood, then this is a pointer to improved lighting. The second natural pointer to action comes from the partners list. Each partner and potential partner has something important to contribute to turning the curve. Systematically consider each partner and their possible contributions.

Look at the research for what has worked in other places including best and promising practice. There is a growing body of work about programs and services that have worked, and important resources on the web. The National Governor's Association and the Rand Corporation websites provide information about best practices. There is much less research on how complex strategies work to produce change in complex environments. The website pathwaystooutcomes.org, a joint project of Harvard University and the Annie E. Casey Foundation, is an excellent resource for considering whole strategies. A more complete list of such resources is given in Appendix J.

Research is important, but it is also important that the thinking of the group not be **limited** by the research. My friends in the academic community sometimes blanch when I say this. But the research world can only tell us a fraction of what we need to know. We've got to make sure we use our own common sense, our own life experience, and our own knowledge of the communities in which we live. Something that has worked somewhere else might not work so well in your community. There must be room for learning and innovation.

Diversity of opinion about what works is a strength, not a deficit. While some agreement will be needed when it comes to allocating resources, there does not have to be a win / lose fight over every action. Some partners will contribute their own money for their part of the action plan and some solutions will involve no-cost or low-cost ideas.

No-cost and Low-cost ideas: Not everything is about money. Some of the most important things you can do sometimes require little or no money. This point was driven home to me during a workshop in El Dorado County, California. In the afternoon of the workshop, we did a turn the curve exercise,[40] where people worked in groups of six to turn a curve that they thought was important. That day people wanted to work on the teen suicide rate. In the preceding two years, there had been an alarming number of teen suicides in El Dorado County. The groups went through the whole RBA thinking process in about an hour. They came back and put their best ideas up on the walls. As we looked around the room at these ideas, half to two thirds of them were no-cost or

---

40.   There are two versions of the Turn the Curve exercise, one about Population Accountability and the other about Performance Accountability. Both versions are given in the Appendix E.

low-cost ideas. They were things that could be done the next day without another dime of money, things like distributing a list of the warning signs of suicide to all the high school students and teachers and providing training in how to recognize and respond to those signs.

This experience led me to another rule. **Any plan that does not have some significant component that is no-cost or low-cost is not complete.** People should be sent back to do more thinking. If you give people permission to think about no-cost and low-cost ideas, you will be amazed at what they come up with. Oddly enough, people need permission to think this way. We have been so thoroughly trained to think about more money for more services, that we are sometimes blind to obvious inexpensive actions that can make a difference.

Information and research agenda about solutions: The second part of the Information and Research Agenda is about what has worked in other places and success stories where people have tackled similar challenges. Again, academic partners can be a great resource in gathering this information. Part of the action plan could include fund raising to commission research that may be needed.[41]

Strategy and Action Plan: Planning without action is meaningless. If you do a good job of thinking about what works, you will come up with more ideas than you can actually do in a year. You will need a set of criteria to set priorities, create an action plan and budget, and get started.

Priority setting is always based on criteria. Sometimes the criteria are explicit, as in review processes for solicited proposals. Sometimes the criteria are implicit, hidden in the preferences and prejudices of the decision makers, as in budget processes. The best group processes use explicit criteria for making choices. Here are four criteria that could be used to select the most powerful actions.[42] Note that the rating process provides an opportunity to fix proposals that get low ratings on any of the criteria. A low leverage proposal can be improved to make it more powerful. A proposal that is not specific enough can be made more specific.

Specificity: Is the idea specific enough to be implemented? Can it actually be done? "Everyone should have housing" is vague and rhetorical. "Building ten new units of low income housing" is a specific action that can be implemented. This is a threshold question, because it is hard to judge an action on the other criteria if it is not specific enough to be accomplished.

Leverage: How much difference will the proposed action make on results, indicators, and turning the curve? This is the most important of the criteria. It doesn't

---

41. My favorite quote about un-needed research was penned on a doctoral dissertation: "Fills a much needed gap in the literature."

42. You can use the pneumonic SILVER to remember these criteria.

matter how well an idea scores on the other criteria if it won't make any difference. Investing in quality child care is a high leverage action to get children ready
for school. Handing out parenting literature at the county fair is not necessarily a
bad idea, but it's a low leverage action.

Values: Is it consistent with our personal and community values? There are many
actions that are specific and high leverage but not consistent with our values. If
you want to improve school attendance rates then kick out all the troublemakers.
If you want to turn the curve on rates of entry into foster care, then slow down or
stop doing investigations of child abuse.[43] These are specific high leverage actions
that will make a difference but should not be done because they're wrong.

Reach[44]: Is it feasible and affordable? Can it actually be done and when? No-cost and
low-cost actions will rate higher here. Actions that require significant new resources
will rate lower. Actions where there is a clear lead person or organization will rate higher.
Actions where everyone says it's a good idea but no one wants to do it will rate lower.

Each proposed action item can be rated "high," "medium" or "low" on each criteria.
The best pattern is obviously HHHH. This pattern is rare. More often you find actions
that are strong on some criteria and weak on others. Consider the action items that rate
highest on specificity, leverage and values, and space them out over a multi-year period.
Actions that rate highest on the first three criteria can be done this year and next year.
Lower rated actions can be done in the next 3 to 5 years.

When this rating process is used with a large group, it is best to do the rating work in
small groups[45] first and then compare the choices of the groups. Often the small groups
will separately identify the same priorities. This convergence of opinion can help develop a larger group consensus. When giving instructions to the small groups, ask for
one person in each group to be the "ombudsman" for the four different criteria. This
helps assure that each criterion is fully considered and helps create a lively debate.

Budget: While you can and should get started with no-cost and low-cost actions, many
of the most important actions will require money. How do you finance an action plan?
Contrary to what you may think, the single most important financing strategy is having a compelling vision. **Powerful visions are magnets for resources.** People with
money want to buy success. The most common financing mistake is to go after the
money first and then figure out what to do with it. In RBA, the vision and action plan

---

43.   There is one state that is reputed to have slowed down child abuse investigations in the
       early 1990's to control foster care caseloads.
44.   The use of the word "reach" here is a deliberate reference to Lisbeth Schorr's *Within Our
       Reach* where she argues that we really know a lot about what works, and our failures are
       most often failures of will and not knowledge.
45.   The ideal size for small group work is 6. It is large enough to provide for diversity of opin-
       ion and small enough that no one can hang back and not participate.

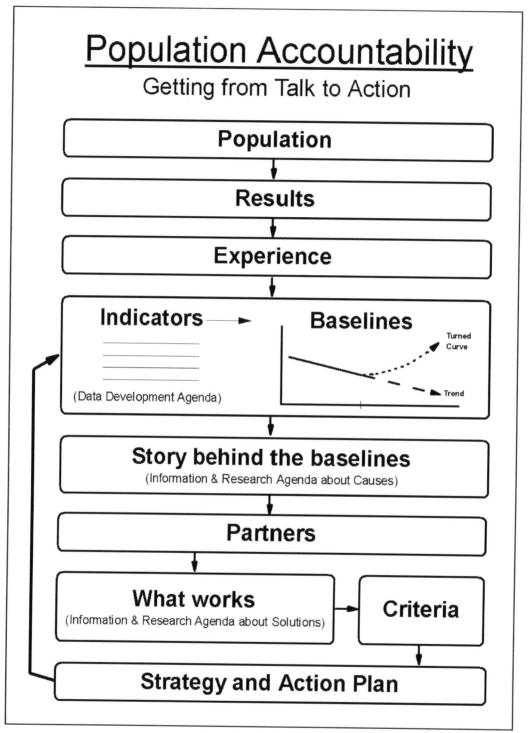

Figure 3.2

The 7 Population Accountability Questions

1. What are the quality of life conditions we want for the children, adults and families who live in our community?

2. What would these conditions look like if we could see them?

3. How can we measure these conditions?

4. How are we doing on the most important of these measures?

5. Who are the partners that have a role to play in doing better?

6. What works to do better, including no-cost and low-cost ideas?

7. What do we propose to do?

Figure 3.3

come first, and financing follows. The second most common mistake is to seek a single source of support for an action plan. People sometimes have had success with only one or two financing strategies, such as getting a foundation grant, or donations from the business community, and they limit their thinking to these approaches. A financing plan must be developed as a **package** of resources. It is a fundamental rule in financing that what you are trying to finance determines where you go for resources. The "Simple Financing Self Assessment" in Appendix I provides a systematic method for thinking broadly about financing options for an action plan.[46]

Considering the talk to action process as a whole: How is the RBA thinking process different from other processes? It's quite simple. RBA takes the definition of success and moves it to the top of the page, in plain language and in measurable terms, and uses that definition of success to drive action plans and budgets. That's not a new method at all. Businesses have been working that way for thousands of years.

This connection between RBA and business was driven home by an experience I had one day in a doctor's office. You know how piles of magazines collect in a doctor's waiting room. That day on the top of the pile next to me was a very fancy publication from Merrill Lynch Associates, stamped CONFIDENTIAL in big red letters. I couldn't resist looking at it. What I found inside was one page per company. Each multi-billion multinational company was reduced to a single page. The top of the page showed the numbers about the company's performance. The middle of the page showed the story behind those numbers: what was happening in the market place, what was happening in the company's management. The conclusion was an action plan, one of three words, "buy, sell or hold."[47] I was worried that this doctor had this confidential document sitting out in his office....so I took it. I dare not reproduce a page here. But there are countless examples of businesses using this same thinking process.

Action items after your first meeting: You can get through the entire RBA thinking process in less than an hour. The Turn the Curve Exercise is one way to do this. RBA does not require 3 months getting step one perfect, and 3 months getting step two perfect, and by the time you get to step three you forgot why you were doing the work in the first place. RBA thinking is designed to be done quickly and then repeated. Each time you repeat the thinking process, your action plan gets better. This means that any group can have an action plan after the first meeting. The first action plan will not be complete, of course. But it's a start. The actions in the first-meeting action plan are usually no-cost and low-cost ideas. As you refine the plan in later meetings and begin to gather resources, the action plan will get better.

What we usually do is skip everything at the beginning of the process and go straight to what works. We have a fight about everyone's favorite program. We di-

---

[46.] For more information on this approach see "The Cosmology of Financing," resultsaccountability.com/publications.

[47.] Thanks to Merrill Lynch for not suing me for describing their report.

vide up whatever money is available. Then three years later we call in an evaluator and ask if the evaluator could please fill in the top of the chart. It's too late. This business of skipping ahead to solutions is very tempting and very common. Much of our political discourse is about means and not ends, about actions and not results. It takes discipline and even a little courage to help a group of partners think about results, indicators and causes, **before** they craft solutions.

The Most Powerful Question: "What would it take to succeed?" This is a better question than "what works?" I believe this is the most powerful question facing our society today. When the Allies invaded Normandy, they did not ask, "What works?" They asked, "What would it take to succeed?" When NASA planned its lunar missions, they thought about what it would take to succeed and they succeeded. We need to bring this same approach to the biggest challenges in our society today. What would it take to end or significantly reduce poverty? What would it take to end or significantly reduce child abuse? What would it take to create a sustainable environment?

The "what would it take?" question is about ambition. Ambitions don't guarantee success, but they make it possible. A sense of ambition shows up in the thinking of Geoffrey Canada, creator of the Harlem Children's Zone. "He wants to prove that poor children, and especially poor black children, can succeed - and not just the smartest or the most motivated or the ones with the most attentive parents, but all of them, in big numbers."[48] This should be the way we all think.

Some people say that it is too hard to reduce teen pregnancy, juvenile crime, and poverty. "Can't we work on something easier?" You can keep picking easier and easier things to work on, and pretty soon you have something easy to do that's not very important. There will always be a need for short term successes but ultimately we will be judged as a society by progress on the big stuff. We will never make progress on the big stuff unless we face it head on and ask "What would it take?"

Research proven practice: I am very troubled by the movement to fund only research-proven practice. This movement's intent to take advantage of proven methods and make the best possible use of scarce dollars is laudable. But there are two problems. First, the research world does not have all the answers. There are many important and powerful ideas that have never been tested by research. If we only fund programs that have been tested, we cut ourselves off from these other ideas. Second, thinking beyond research is often the most creative edge of the work. We must allow for the exploration of new ideas and the development of new knowledge. I have no problem with giving preference to research, but we must also allow research to be adapted to the unique circumstances of each community, and we must give people room to experiment and learn.

---

48.   New York Times Magazine, June 20, 2004.

Core strategies vs. result-specific strategies: Many if not most actions contribute to more than one result.[49] Creating a community center could help make the community safer, help children succeed in school, and help parents get jobs. Groups that are working on more than one result at a time should identify the core strategies that cut across results and those that are specific to one result. Written plans can be coded to show core actions that may deserve a higher priority in developing the action plan.

Where do you start? It doesn't matter where you start. Start anywhere. Start where the passion is. Whatever you do will have beneficial effects across a range of results. Con Hogan, former Secretary of the Vermont Agency of Human Services, has a great way to summarize this: **"Anywhere leads to everywhere."** If you improve the teen pregnancy rate you will also improve the high school graduation rate. If you reduce teen smoking you will impact rates of low birthweight babies. All of these conditions of well-being are tightly interconnected. Touch the web anywhere and the effects are felt throughout.

How to choose population results

Choosing results is as much a political process as it is a technical process. What set of statements captures the most important hopes for our children, families, community, city, county, state or nation?

One way to elicit this from a group is to put the following unfinished sentences on the board:

- We want children who are...
- We want families that are...
- We want to live in a nation, state, county, city or community that is...

The group is asked to complete these sentences with adjectives descriptive of well-being. For example, "We want children who are safe, happy, confident and ready for school." "We want families that are safe, stable, connected, self sufficient." "We want to live in a community that is clean and safe, where neighbors know each other." Each completed sentence is a result. After the group lists its ideas, three small groups can be formed to edit these down to a shorter, more easily communicated list. The children's group is asked to produce 5 statements. The family group is asked to produce 3 statements. The community group is asked to produce 2 statements. At the end of about two hours, there is a list of 10 results that represents the group's consensus.[50]

There are three elements that are typically found in broadly based processes that have successfully developed results and indicators.

---

49. This is one of the consequences of the non-linear relationship between Population and Performance Accountability.

50. This process is more fully described in the exercise "A Results List from Scratch," in Appendix F.

- There is a sponsoring group that consists of high level, well respected leaders. In Georgia, the Family and Children's Policy Council that developed Georgia's results for children and families had leaders from the legislature, the governor's cabinet, the business community and the faith community.
- If you pick the right leaders, they won't have time to do the work themselves. There must be staff to support the leadership group. This is anywhere from a half-time person to 5 or more staff. The leadership considers the staff's recommendations and creates a working list of results and indicators.
- The leadership group sponsors an inclusive comment process with public hearings and focus groups. The leadership group considers this input, makes adjustments to their initial proposals, and issues a "final" list of results.

Figure 3.4 shows examples of results that come from these kind of processes. Notice that these are very different in content and style, but in each case they are plain language statements of well-being.

Avoid referencing services in results statements: One of the most important characteristics of a well constructed population result statement is that it is not about data

Examples of Results		
Georgia	**Placer County, California**[51]	**Vermont** (First tier outcomes from Act 186)
1. Healthy chidlren 2. Children ready for school 3. Children succeeding in school 4. Strong families 5. Self-sufficient families	1. Safe 2. Healthy 3. At home 4. In School 5. Out of trouble	1. Vermont has a prosperous economy. 2. Vermonters are healthy. 3. Vermont's environment is clean and sustainable. 4. Vermont's communities are safe and supportive. 5. Vermont's families are safe, nurturing, stable, and supported. 6. Vermont's children and young people achieve their potential 7. Vermont's elders and people with disabilities and people with mental conditions live with dignity and independence in settings they prefer. 8. Vermont has open, effective, and inclusive government at the State and local levels.

Figure 3.4

---

51. See David Gray's excellent book: *Safe, Healthy, At Home, In School and Out of Trouble: Making child and family services work for children and families*, 2004.

and not about service. In the RBA framework, the need for data is addressed by indicators, and services are best considered as means and not ends.

People often propose results that make reference to a specific service. One of the most common is "All pre-school children receive high quality child care."[52] Whenever you use this kind of statement as a starting point for the RBA process, it quickly leads to not-very-helpful circular thinking.

> **Result**: All children receive high quality child care
> **Indicator**: Percent of children who receive high quality child care
> **Story**: Not enough high quality child care
> **What works**: More high quality child care.

It is better to think of any service, no matter how important, as a means, not an end in itself. So, in this case, child care can and should be part of the discussion of what works to advance the result *All children ready for school*.

The same rule against referencing services in results statements also applies to indicators. If the indicator is "percent of people receiving service" then the same circular thinking leads to a strategy to provide more of that service. Service thinking alone is too narrow to produce a good action plan. Getting children ready for school, for example, will require the contributions of many partners that are not part of the formal service system such as parents, grandparents, the business community, and the media.

One immediate benefit of this shift in thinking is that it puts advocacy for that particular service on a different and more solid footing. Rather that arguing that child care is a good in and of itself, the argument shifts to how child care contributes to the higher purpose of assuring that all children are ready for and succeeding in school. Child care becomes more than just another service competing for money, but part of a larger strategy to achieve something everyone can readily support. It provides space for us to think deeply about other actions required to achieve these ends. We remove a burden that is unfairly placed on child care as the only path to school readiness and school success for children.

This same shift in emphasis can strengthen advocacy for other services. Instead of arguing for more child protection staff, frame the discussion around child safety. If the public accepts the importance of child safety, they will be more likely to support funding for programs that promote safety.[53]

Another way in which services are referenced in results statements involves a description of the intended quality of government services. For example, one county sets out

---

52. Not all child care is created equal, and when the term child care is used here, it refers to high quality child care.

53. This is not much different from the ancient rules of advertising, where you must first convince people they need new clothes, a car or golf clubs, before offering up the particular one you want them to buy.

Modern and Responsive County Government as one of several population results. This is arguably a result, since it is a condition of well-being for people in a geographic area. The problem is that virtually every piece of data that describes this condition will be a performance measure for the county service system. This blurs the line between Population and Performance Accountability and runs the risk that people will see good county services as an end and not a means. The better way to handle this is to produce documents that have clearly separate sections on Population Accountability that address the quality of life for all people in the area and Performance Accountability that address the performance of the people's government and its programs. This can be illustrated by the difference between two questions: "How is the city doing?" vs. "How is the city government doing?" In Chapter 6 we will look at budgeting and planning formats that clearly separate Population and Performance Accountability.

As you might expect, there are exceptions to these rules. In much of the world, education services are severely restricted for young girls and women.[54] The numbers and percent of young girls and women eligible for and participating in the education system becomes every bit as important as the educational results themselves. There are times when the availability of an important service is a kind of result. However, this construction should be avoided whenever possible.

Another common mistake is to structure the quality of life report card using service headings like: Health, Education, Environment, and Safety. People sometimes think these are results, but they are not. Health, Education, Environment and Safety are categories of service or labels for the organizational components of government. Using government service and organizational categories reinforces the old way of thinking that pins responsibility for a population condition on one agency. The solution to this problem is quite simple:

> Instead of "Health" use *All Children and Adults are Physically and Mentally Healthy.*
> Instead of "Education" use *All Children are Ready for and Succeed in School.*
> Instead of "Environment" use *A Clean and Sustainable Environment.*
> Instead of "Safety" use *Safe Communities.*

The difference in wording may not seem like much, but the underlying message is very important. When true results statements are used, it is much easier to see that responsibility for progress does not, and cannot, rest with any one department of government or even with government alone. Results have tremendous power to motivate people and bring people together. Services categories do not.

Another common problem with result statements has to do with the words "improve, increase and decrease." Consider the result *Improved High School Graduation*. There are two problems here. First, the statement implicitly references the high school gradua-

---

54. This is a major priority of the UN World Population Fund and statistics are available from their website.

tion rate. Data statements are always best addressed as indicators, not results. Secondly, the word "improve" may signal a lower level of ambition than the group intends. What if the graduation rate goes from 50% to 51%? This passes the test for improvement, but is certainly not what anyone hopes to achieve. A better and simpler construction would be to make the result: *All Children Succeed in School* and one of the indicators the high school graduation rate. The use of the word "all" is optional, but it signals that our ambition is for all children to succeed, that it is not OK for us to allow some children to fail. This does not mean that we expect to fully achieve this ambition. We will get incrementally closer by turning the curve on the high school graduation rate. But the most important statement of our purpose is not limited by settling for the achievement of a particular percent or amount of increase.

Avoid the "King of the Hill" syndrome where one result is given pre-eminent importance over all others. In one county, the county commissioners authorized a significant effort to advance *Family Self Sufficiency.* A range of other results (*Children are Healthy and Safe,* etc.) were then identified as subordinate to self-sufficiency. Clearly health and safety both contribute to family self-sufficiency. But self-sufficiency also contributes to health and safety. When any one result is designated as the most important, all other results can be viewed as subordinate contributors. This relationship is artificial and unhelpful. When more than one result is articulated, it is better to view them as co-equal, not hierarchical.

Avoid creating multiple levels of results: Aside from the artifice of one pre-eminent result, there are situations where lists of results have two (or even three) levels. So for example:

> Level 1 Result: Clean Environment
> Level 2 Result: Clean Air
> Level 2 Result: Clean Water

Each level is a plain language statement of well-being. But multiple layers make the work more complicated. People sometimes further confound the situation by calling the different levels by different names. Level 1 results are called "Results." But level 2 results are called something else such as "Objectives," or "Goals." Since both Level 1 and Level 2 are actually conditions of well-being, per our definition of results above, the introduction of another label for this same idea completely undermines any chance for discipline in language and thinking.

From a practical standpoint, it is best to avoid all this complexity by having one level of results and then using indicators to address what would otherwise be a second or third level. The example above would become:

> Result 1: Clean Environment
> > Indicator 1: Percent of days with clean air
> > Indicator 2: Percent of stream miles meeting water quality standards

Clarity and simplicity are virtues in choosing results and indicators.

How to choose indicators to measure results

For each result, there is a set of indicators that reflect the extent to which the result is being achieved. Figure 3.5 shows some examples of indicators:

Notice the differences between how these very similar results are measured. Montgomery County uses five measures. Vermont uses eight. Only one measure (rate of substantiated child abuse and neglect) is used in both places. Vermont lists poverty statistics here while Montgomery County lists the poverty rate under a separate result: *Economic Self-Sufficiency.* Both lists are powerful and appropriate. There is not a right or wrong set of measures for any given result. Choosing indicators will always be a matter of judgment and compromise, and different groups will come up with different answers about what indicators to use.

How do you choose the best indicators to represent a result? Any choice can be reduced to a set of criteria. The following three criteria have been used to choose indicators in many places.

Examples of Indicators	
Montgomery Co. Ohio[55]	**Vermont[56]** (Pre Act 186)
Result: Stable Families **Indicators:** 1. Percent of first births where both parents completed high school, parents are married (at any time from conception to birth), and the mother is at least 20 years old. 2. **Rate of substantiated child abuse and neglect.** 3 & 4. Deaths to children ages 0 - 17 that were ruled preventable, or somewhat preventable, by the Child Fatality Review Board. 5. Domestic violence deaths.	**Result**: Children live in Stable Supported Families **Indicators:** 1. Percent of children in poverty. 2. Percent of children in families receiving food stamps. 3. Percent of child support paid. 4. Percent of parentage established for out-of-wedlock child support cases. 5. **Rate of substantiated child abuse and neglect.** 6. Percent of children ages 5 - 17 in families receiving welfare. 7. Rate of out-of-home placements. 8. Average number of moves within the child substitute care system.

Figure 3.5

---

[55]. Montgomery County Family and Children First Council, 2004 Progress Report, Outcomes, Indicators and Strategic Community Initiatives, December 2004.

[56]. Vermont Agency of Human Services, *2004 Community Profiles*, January 2005, ahs.state.vt.us.

Communication Power: Does the indicator communicate to a broad and diverse audience? This criteria is sometimes called the *public square test.* If you had to stand in a public square[57] and explain the result to your neighbors, what two or three pieces of data would be the most powerful? Obviously you could bring a thick report and begin a long recitation. The crowd would thin out fast. It is hard for people to listen to more than a few pieces of data at one time. The data must be common sense, and compelling. The crime rate has communication power. The rate of successful adjudication does not.

Proxy Power (or Representation Power): Does the indicator say something of central importance about the result? Can this measure stand as a proxy or representative for the plain language statement of well-being? We know, for example, that the percent of children reading at grade level in the 3rd grade is a powerful measure of school success. Children who can't read in 3rd grade have a much higher chance of failing in later grades and dropping out of school. So 3rd grade reading scores are a powerful proxy for the result *All Children Succeed in School."*

The other part of proxy power has to do with the fact that **data tend to run in herds**. If one indicator is going in the right direction, usually others are as well. You do not need 20 indicators telling you the same thing. Pick the indicators that have the greatest proxy power, specifically those that are most likely to match the direction of the other indicators in the herd.

Data Power: Do we have quality data on a timely basis? Is the data reliable and consistent? To what extent do we have the data at the state, county, city and community levels?[58]

Each indicator is rated High, Medium or Low (H-M-L) on each criteria. We are looking for indicators that rank high on all three criteria. These are indicators that communicate well, that tell us something of central importance about the result, for which good data is available. If we can find indicators that have these three characteristics, there's a good chance they will work with our neighbors in the public square.

There are two messages in this rating system. The first message is "Start with the best of what you have." The second message is "Get better."

---

57.   Or perhaps the central atrium of your local shopping mall.

58.   Some places prefer to use a larger list of criteria, or phrase the criteria differently. In almost every case, these separate criteria are components of Communication, Proxy and Data power. For example, one county split Data power into four separate criteria: Valid, Available, Accurate, and Reliable. The same county thought "communication power" sounded too much like jargon. So they renamed it "Easily understood." This is all good. Whatever works.

Data is often used as an excuse, "We could be accountable for the children in our community when we have better data." If we are honest, we will admit that we said that 10 years ago. We'll say it again 10 years from now. **Do not make the collection of new data a precondition for getting started.**[59] You have to start with the data you have. In fact, only by starting with the data you have do you have any chance of generating the support you need to get better data.

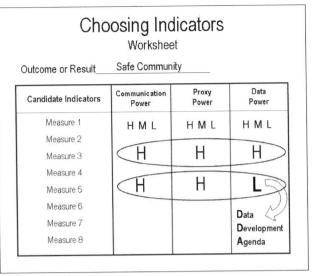

Figure 3.6

These three criteria lead to a three-part indicator list **for each result:**

Primary or Headline Indicators: The 3 to 5 most important measures. These are the ones you have data for that rise to the top in the rating process.

Secondary Indicators: Any other measures for which there is good data. We do not throw away good data. We will use these measures in assessing the story behind the baselines, and other parts of the process.

Data Development Agenda: The priorities for new and improved data.

This is not a process that is done once and is then finished. This is a living, changing list. As you develop new and better data, you may promote one measure to become a primary indicator and demote another measure to become a secondary indicator.

Note that there is a newer shortcut version of this rating system that is easier to use than the H-M-L method described above. After brainstorming possible measures, circle the ones for which you have good data (Data power). Then ask, "If you could use only three of these measures in the public square, which would be your first, second and third choices?" This question combines Communication power and Proxy power into a single step, and yields headline and secondary measures. Then ask, "Of the ones for which you do not have data, which would be the first, second and third ones you would buy?" This yields the Data Development Agenda. (See Appendix G for more information on this method.)

---

59.   The RBA process can be started without any data at all. Groups can use the results and experience to drive the thinking process. Groups can also create working versions of indicator baselines based on group consensus about history and what the future will look like if we don't change. See Appendix F.

Baselines and the definition of success

Like other words in this book, the word "baseline" has many possible meanings. RBA uses a definition that comes from the budget world. Budget baselines have two parts: an historical part that tells us where we've been, and a forecast part that shows where we're headed if we don't do something more or different than what we are doing now.

Creating the forecast part of a baseline is an art, not a science.[60] There is not a single, right forecast. It is sometimes useful to show a range of forecast scenarios: high, medium, and low; or optimistic, pessimistic, and most likely.

As chief financial officer of the Maryland Department of Human Resources, I was responsible for overseeing the department's forecasts of welfare caseloads, child support collections, foster care caseloads and child abuse and child neglect reports. These forecasts were needed to estimate the department's staffing requirements and the end-of-year surplus or deficit. Each quarter, we updated our forecasts through the end of the current and succeeding fiscal years. We tempered our review of the numbers with what we knew about policy changes, developments in the 24 local Departments of Social Services, and what was happening on the street. The best forecasting work is based on this kind of open learning process.

Not all forecasts are straight lines. In economic forecasting, periods of growth are followed by periods of decline. Economic forecasts almost always involve estimating when the current period of growth or decline will slow down and turn in the other direction. Straight line forecasts also don't apply when the numbers in the historical part of the baseline are very small. For example, the number of suicides in a small geographic area often go up and down without any clear pattern. The forecast in this case might be a continuation of the up and down pattern in the same range. In Boston, the number of juvenile homicides ranged from 6 to 16 over a six year period in the late 1980's and early 1990's. While it was not possible to predict exactly where this line would go, there was little argument that it would continue in this range if something was not done to change it.

We are finding more and more reports that present the historical part of baselines but not the forecast part. The forecast part is essential for two reasons. First, it allows us to ask and answer the questions, "Is this future OK?" "Juvenile crime has been rising in our community. If we don't do something about it, this is where we're headed, folks. Is that OK?" "Water quality has been declining. If we don't do something about it, this is where we're headed. Is that OK?"

---

60.   One of my favorite Yogi Berra quotes comes from one year in the 1950's, before the World Series, when Yogi was asked to forecast his performance in the upcoming series. He hesitated for a second and said, "You know forecasting is really difficult... especially about the future."

If people say "Yeah, that's OK with me," then you have no basis to move from talk to action. The first step in getting from talk to action is for someone to say, "That's **not OK,** we could do better." Stephen Covey talks about "pain and vision" as the ingredients of change.[61] The forecast of an unacceptable future is the pain part of the equation.

The other reason why baselines with forecasts are so important is that they allow us to define suc-cess as **turning the curve** away

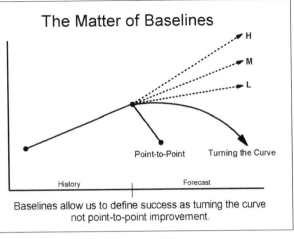

The Matter of Baselines

Baselines allow us to define success as turning the curve
not point-to-point improvement.

Figure 3.7

from the baseline or beating the baseline. This is a very common sense idea that we see all the time in the rest of the world. The U.S. Congressional Budget Office routinely forecasts policy-neutral estimates of federal deficits against which tax and spending proposals are debated. Similar forecasting occurs routinely in business planning.

In most work in the government and non-profit sectors, success is not defined this way. Success usually means **point to point** improvement, moving from where we are now to a new better place. Crime should go down. High school graduation should go up. Every measure has a success direction and success is moving to a new place in that direction. "We will be successful if crime is reduced by 20% in the next two years." "Our school will be successful if reading scores go up by 5% per year."

The problem is that the world doesn't work that way. Most conditions we are trying to change have a history. They have momentum. Often the trend has been headed in the wrong direction for a long time. Sometimes the best you can do is slow down the rate at which things are getting worse, before you can flatten the curve and turn it in the right direction.[62] Every time we define success as point to point improvement, it is a setup for failure. Two years later, if we haven't hit the new lower (or higher) level, our work is declared a failure and we go on to the next fad. If we are serious about this work, we have to be more business-like about it. And business-like means using base-lines and the concept of turning the curve to define success.

Some people argue that the notion of turning the curve is too complicated and takes too long to work in a political environment. Impatience, driven by term limits and the frequent turnover of elected officials, has made the demand for short term improve-

---

61. I'm pretty sure he said this.
62. The idea of turning the curve does not depend on the baselines headed in the wrong di-rection. If the baseline is headed in the right direction, then turning the curve means ac-celerating the rate of improvement.

ment even stronger. However, most elected leaders want a way to assess the big picture, whether or not we, as city, county, state or nation are really making progress. Is all this money we're spending on programs getting us somewhere? Baselines can help answer this question. The political need for short term accomplishments will never change. But we can add a systematic way of assessing if all this short term activity adds up to longer term progress.

Baseline curves don't always take a long time to turn. Changes in program performance measures and population indicators can happen much more quickly than people think. If you look at the stories in this book about Boston's work on juvenile homicide, or Tillamook County's work on teen pregnancy, you can see significant progress in 15 to 18 months.

One common mistake in creating baselines is to forecast where you want to go instead of where you think you're headed if you don't do something different. The purpose of the baseline forecast is to establish what a policy-neutral or budget-neutral future might look like, so that the discussion can focus on whether proposed actions will make things better or worse than this future. The policy-neutral path should always be clearly differentiated from the policy-change path.

Of course, any framework can be misused. In one county, a department of county government was trying to sell the county council on more money for a teen pregnancy prevention program. So they drew a chart with the history of teen pregnancy rates and two alternative forecasts. The first forecast, labeled "without investment" made a sharp, almost 90 degree turn upwards. The second forecast labeled "with investment" made an equally sharp turn in the other direction. It was a joke. Nobody believed either forecast. I don't remember if they got the money or not. But they should have been embarrassed. And I was embarrassed because they said they were using RBA.

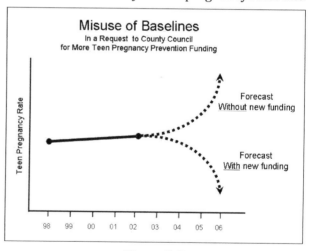

Figure 3.8

Baseline forecasts must be credible, otherwise the process collapses. It is important to involve key stakeholders in the creation of credible forecasts. Most states, counties and cities have formal forecasting processes for important revenue and expense components of the budget. In Florida, there is a joint executive and legislative branch committee that establishes projections for revenue and for key non-discretionary expenditures. This expertise exists in most state and local jurisdictions to one degree or another. Building a consensus on the forecast of "what will happen if we don't do something different," will pay dividends later in the process. It lays the groundwork for the discussion about what needs to be done.

Quality of life report cards

Once a set of results and indicators has been developed, it is possible to create an annual report card for a city, county, state or nation. Looking at this kind of report card is like looking in a mirror. People see whether the community's quality of life is getting better or worse. Sometimes people look at the report card and they don't like what they see. This can be the first step in bringing people together to take action.[63]

Such report cards have been developed for dozens, perhaps hundreds of cities, counties and communities across the United States and in other countries. There are many different ways to construct a report card, but the best ones use a structure based on results and indicators. Vermont has produced some of the best work. The excerpt from the Vermont 2001 report (Figure 3.9) shows two facing pages for one of Vermont's outcomes.[64] The left side shows "Heartening Indicators," "Troublesome Indicators," and the "Story behind the curve." The second page shows the action plan in two parts: accomplishments from last year and recommended actions for next year. This is a brilliant construction that puts all the essential information for each outcome in a format that every community member can understand.

In 1991, the Annie E. Casey Foundation issued the first Kids Count report comparing all 50 states and the District of Columbia on 8 indicators of child and family well-being. Kids Count has grown to include a network of state partners that now issue reports for counties (and sometimes cities) within their states. These reports have helped to create a national movement toward regular periodic assessment of indicators of child and family well-being. Links to the Kids Count reports can be found on aecf.org. A partial list of exemplary report cards on child and family well-being includes those found in Contra Costa County, Los Angeles County, Marin County, San Mateo County, Santa Clara County, and Santa Cruz County, California; Montgomery County, Ohio; Philadelphia, Pennsylvania; and at both the state and local levels in Georgia, Oregon and Vermont. Links to other exemplary children's report cards can been found on raguide.org.

---

63. See "Bringing people together to do this work" in Chapter 7.
64. "Outcome-Based Planning: State Partners and Local Communities Working Together to Improve the Well-Being of All Vermonters: A Report from the State Team for Children, Families and Individuals," Vermont Agency of Human Services, February, 2001.

State Team Outcome # 5

Children Live in Stable and Supported Families

Heartening Indicators:

Young Teen Pregnancy Rate
Estimated pregnancies per 1,000 girls aged 15-17

Year 2010 Goal
U.S.
Vermont

About 1 in 48 Vermont girls 15 to 17 years old became pregnant in 1999.

Child Abuse & Neglect
Substantiated Victims

Vermont

Percent of Child Support Cases with Collections

Vermont
U.S.

The Story Behind the Curve

- Teen pregnancy rates have improved with expanded access to health care, heightened attention to the role of men in pregnancy prevention, and community-based teen pregnancy programs.
- There has been a significant decline in child abuse and neglect. A major effort by the Department of Social and Rehabilitation Services to encourage reporting, coupled with a broadening of policy in "risk-of-harm" cases, has resulted in an increase in both reports and victims in the past 12 months.
- Child support collections have had significant increases related to an excellent automation system, mandatory wage withholding, law, and the ability to attach assets.

Troublesome Indicators:

New Families at Risk
Percent of New births

U.S.
Vermont

"First births to unmarried women younger than 20, with fewer than 12 years' education.

Average Number of Moves per Child in Substitute Care

Total Bed Nights of People Housed in Temporary Shelters in Vermont

59,972	67,350	63,111
FY 98	FY 99	FY 2000

The Story Behind the Curve

- New families remain at risk when moms under 20 have babies, babies are born to single mothers, and the mother lacks a high school diploma.
- Children in custody move more frequently due to an increase and intensity of challenging behaviors.
- The lack of availability and affordability of housing continues to affect the number of people housed in temporary shelters in Vermont.

#5: Children Live in Stable and Supported Families

Recommendations	Accomplishments in 2000	Recommendations for 2001	Actions/Strategies 2001
Families achieve economic independence	• Conference on "living assets project" held in 2/2000 included in Welfare Reform legislation. • Community Action Program agencies distributed livable wage information. • CAP agencies, the Department of Prevention, Assistance, Transition and Health Access and Headstart distributed information about earned income tax credit.	*Families live in safe and affordable housing*	• Provide supports to help keep people in their homes. • Provide case management services to support high-risk tenants. • Promote affordable housing in all local planning initiatives.
Families are partners in developing support and direct services	• Vermont Federation of Families are now operating in seven regions of the state. • Parent to Parent has regional capacity. • The Parent-Child Centers have been doing *Parents As Teachers* and outreach to families about how services work. • Interagency Training Committee began developing information to ensure accommodations and support for parents with disabilities. This will be continued and enhanced by the Green Mountain Family Network Grant. • Victim Advocacy programs have been strengthened. • The Legislature requested a substance abuse prevention intervention and treatment framework from the Department of Health for January, 2001. • All regions of the State have Community Resource Guides in hand copy and on the internet. • Eight Parent Leadership programs are in operation. • There is an SRS Consumer Advisory Board in operation in each region. • Six Regional Partnerships were funded for family involvement through the Family Consortium and the remaining Regional Partnerships are now applying for Green Mountain Family Network grants in the second round.	*Families are supported by their communities*	• Provide better parenting support for incarcerated parents and support their transition back to their families. • Support and enhance the role of fathers in their children' lives. • Family organizations expand connections with Regional Partnerships. • Vermont Federation of Families will continue to expand family resource consultants to all regions. • Strengthen the collaboration of families, court personnel and service providers with an annual "Meet the Judge" opportunity. • Encourage hiring of experienced family members in peer support and mentor roles. • Increase the number of services and activities associated with afterschool programs. • Determine effective ways to support the parents of preteens in promoting positive youth development. • Green Mountain Network/Children's UPstream Services (CUPS) Family Consortium grants will expand family networks to all regions.

Figure 3.9

WHERE RESULTS-BASED ACCOUNTABILITY
THINKING HAS WORKED

Vermont[65]

One of the places that has made the most progress using Results-Based Accountability is Vermont. In the early 1990's, Vermont identified ten "outcomes" for children, families and communities, and began issuing report cards, known as Community Profiles. The profiles were produced for each of the 59 school districts in the state and showed baselines for over 70 indicators, organized by the state's ten outcomes.[66] The reports were produced by the Vermont Agency of Human Services in partnership with the Vermont Department of Education.

Vermont established the State Team for Children, Families and Individuals, to work on improving outcomes across the state.[67] Membership on the State Team included a balance of state agency staff and representatives from the state's 12 regional partnerships. The State Team had 10 standing subcommittees, one for each of the ten outcomes. The subcommittees took turns reporting to the larger group over ten meetings per year. Each of the regional partnerships had a similar process to track indicator data, organize partners and take action. This state-local partnership laid the groundwork for a later executive branch - legislative branch - nonprofit partnership. which came together around the need for common language and common accountability methods. Act 186 placed an amended set of outcomes into state law and incorporated an RBA approach to accountability at both the population and performance levels. Over the years, Vermont has pro-

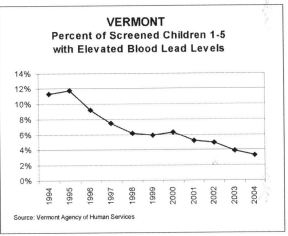

Figure 3.10

---

duced significant improvements in many of the state's indicators. with many Turn the Curve stories to tell. Here is one of them.

Vermont is a small state of only 630,000 people. The state has a high percent of older housing stock, particularly in rural areas. Many of the houses constructed prior to 1978 contained lead paint, which is especially toxic to toddlers and young children who ingest paint peelings and dust. Lead poisoning is known to have life-long damaging effects on a child's mental and physical development. Over time, the indicator "Lead Levels in Children" remained stubbornly unacceptable.

By the early 1990's there were several public health education efforts geared to bringing more awareness to this issue. In 1991, the state and local partnerships decided to include a focus on lead paint in their new strategic effort to visit the homes of families with newborn babies. These visits were designed to offer information, provide opportunities to sign up for needed services, and help create social connections for young families who often lead isolated lives.

Every family with a newborn (there are about 6,000 births per year in Vermont) was offered a visit by someone trained to make these visits. The family "visitors" came from different institutions depending on the district. In one district, the visitor was a school nurse. In other districts, a public health nurse or community volunteer played this role.

One of the conversations that occurred during these visits concerned lead paint.

> *Was this house built before the 1980's? If so, may we look at the paint around some of the windows? Are there any paint chips around these window that have come loose over the years? It is very likely that some of these chips may have been ground into dust over time, and it is also likely that your young toddler may be ingesting some of this lead filled dust. May we arrange for a lead screening for your child? There is a state lead abatement program that exists to help take care of problems like this. Would you like us to connect you with that program?*

In addition to lead levels, a number of other indicators were expected to improve as a result of home visiting and related community efforts, including 2 year immunization rates, abuse rates for young children, and children's health coverage. Over time, the larger strategy of offering visits to families with newborns contributed strongly to turned indicator curves in these areas. Eighty eight percent of families accepted the home visits. In the case of the percent of children ages 1-5 with elevated lead levels, the curve turned dramatically, dropping from 11.3% in 1994 to 5.9% in 1999. The state percentages dropped significantly faster than national totals during this period, cutting the gap from approximately 6.9 percentage points in 1994 to approximately 3.3 percentage points in 1999-2000.[68]

---

[68]. The percent of children 1 to 5 in the United States with elevated lead levels in their blood (above 10 ug/dL) was 4.4% for 1991 - 1994 and 2.2% for 1999-2000 according to the CDC National Health and Nutrition Examination Surveys (NHANES).

Vermont No-cost and Low-cost Stories

Vermont also offers some good examples of where no-cost and low-cost actions made a difference.

In the mid 1990's, Medicaid costs were rising rapidly in Vermont as they were in the rest of country. One of the largest components of Medicaid is nursing home care for elderly and disabled individuals. In one region of the state, these costs were growing much faster than in the rest of the state. The state asked the local regional partnership to bring people together to see why this was happening and what could be done to slow the rate of nursing home entries. As an added incentive, the state offered to share some of the Medicaid savings with the local group if the rate of increase could be slowed. The group soon discovered that one of the leading causes of entry into nursing care was hip fractures. This is a very serious injury for an older person. Often it is not possible for the person to return home after their hospital stay and nursing care becomes the only option. The group dug deeper into the story behind the curve. The group soon discovered that one of the leading causes of these falls was... winter. Elders were slipping on the ice and snow. The group decided to organize a community-wide effort to shovel the walks of the older people in the community.

Another community with a similar challenge organized something they called "drive by shoveling." After a snow storm, three or four students and one teacher from the high school would drive around the town. If they found an un-shoveled walk, they would jump out, shovel the walk, get back in the car and drive off.

Still another no-cost effort involved the young people who served as baggers at the local grocery store. If an older person came through the line, they were asked to look down and see if the older person's shoelaces were untied. If the laces were untied, the young people were asked to get down on their hands and knees and tie them. No money was attached to any of these efforts. To my knowledge there is not yet a federal shoelace program. They represent the kind of common sense no-cost and low-cost contributions that everyday citizens can make to advance the well-being of their community.

Chapter 4:

PERFORMANCE ACCOUNTABILITY
For Programs, Agencies and Service Systems

In this chapter, we address the second half of the Results-Based Accountability framework: Performance Accountability or how managers and their partners can improve the performance of programs, agencies and service systems.

The methods in this chapter allow managers to begin using performance measures right away, without spending time filling out logic model forms or other preliminaries. The basic premise is this: Most managers know how their program works. They should be able to identify the three to five most important measures for their program, explain how the program is doing on those measures, and present what can be done to improve the program's performance.

Our exploration of Performance Accountability starts with an examination of the mental models we use to think about performance measurement. Then we look at a simple yet complete way to categorize performance measures and a 7 Question talk to action process that any manager can use to improve performance.

The change-agent vs. industrial models:

Much of the tradition of performance measurement comes from the industrial part of the private sector. Industrial processes turn raw materials into finished products. The raw materials are the inputs; the finished products are the outputs. Some of the very first work on performance measurement were the time and motion studies in the late 19th and early 20th centuries that looked at how to improve worker productivity and industrial production.

This model makes sense for organizations that make things, but it does not translate very well to public or private sector organizations that provide services.[69] It does not seem right to think of clients, workers, supplies and office space as inputs to the service sausage machine, producing outputs of cured, served or fixed clients. The implication that there is a mechanistic relationship between inputting staff resources and outputting customer benefits seems absurd, if not insulting to teachers, health care

---

[69.] It is important to note that performance work in the private sector, including the industrial sector, has gone beyond the simple model noted here. The intent here is not to set up private industry as a straw man, but to suggest that many public and private agencies are stuck with performance models that don't serve them well.

workers, police officers and other service providers. Industrial model proponents have tried to patch up this problem by adding the word outcome to describe a more important type of output, but the conceptual problems remain. Working with people is simply more complicated than working with machines. We need a different image and a different language to describe this work. You are not a machine on the factory floor. None of the people who work with you are machines on the factory floor.

While most industrialized countries have shifted to a service and information economy, the image of our work remains a vestige of the industrial past. It is time to throw off the chains of the industrial model and begin using a mental model that is more appropriate to the provision of services. That alternative is the change-agent model. When your program works well, you and your colleagues are change-agents, not machines. In the change-agent model, the program provides services (effort) that lead to changes in the well-being of clients, families, or communities (effect).

One common situation illustrates the problems that arise when industrial model thinking is applied to change-agent services. It is the belief that the number of clients served is an output or product of the service, "We have assembled workers (input); and we are in the business of processing un-served clients (another input) into served clients (output)." This odd application of industrial performance concepts captures much of what is wrong with the way we think about service performance today. In the change-agent model, the "number of clients served" is not an end product. Serving clients is a means to a change in customer or social conditions, the true end or purpose of the work.

A closely related industrial model problem involves treating dollars spent as inputs, and clients served as outputs. In this view, dollars are the raw materials, and what the program does with those dollars are outputs. It's easy to see why this fails to meet the public's need for accountability. In this construct, the fact that an agency spent all the money it received is a type of performance accountability. This is surely a form of intellectual if not literal bankruptcy.

The shift to change-agent thinking is more important than it may sound. The concept of change agent resonates with the purposes of service delivery more than the concept of cogs and gears. We cannot expect people to embrace industrial measurement categories that carry an implicit message of disrespect. Change-agent thinking fits better with what service workers actually do. Further, performance methods derived from the change-agent model are more likely to be seen as an aid to service delivery and not an intrusion or threat.

Three simple performance measure categories:
How much did we do? How well did we do it? Is anyone better off?

Any Performance Accountability system is defined by the way performance measures are categorized, selected and used. Let's start with how we categorize performance measures.

All performance measures that have ever existed for any program in the history of the universe can be derived from thinking about the quantity and quality of effort and effect.

The distinction between quantity and quality is familiar: how much we did versus how well we did it. Some people think that quantity can be measured and quality can't be measured. The quality of a program and its services **can** be measured and throughout this chapter we will present measures for both quantity and quality.

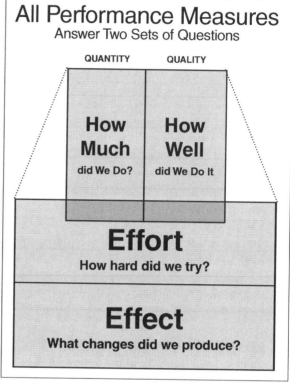

Figure 4.1

The distinction between effort and effect is simply the difference between how hard we tried and whether we made a difference in the lives of our customers.

Figure 4.1 shows how these two different perspectives are combined to produce the following categories:

Quantity of effort: How much service was provided?

Quality of effort: How well was the service provided?

Quantity of effect: How many customers are better off?

Quality of effect: What percent of customers are better off and how are they better off?

Figure 4.2 shows how these combinations lead to the three universal performance measurement categories: *How much did we do? How well did we do it? Is anyone better off?*

Let's consider some different programs and how their measures fit into these categories. In each case, the measures for the given program are examples and not a complete list. The programs are chosen to show how these categories can be applied broadly across the public and private/nonprofit sectors.

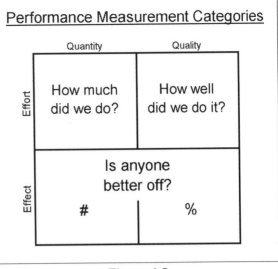

Figure 4.2

It's easiest to start with **education**, because everyone has experience with the education system. Measures for *How much did we do?* include the number of students served, number of teachers, hours of instruction and dollars spent. Measures for *How well did we do it?* include the student-teacher ratio, the retention rate for highly qualified teachers, and the percent of school buildings in need of significant repair.

We can teach students with highly qualified teachers at a low ratio in a nice building, and we still haven't answered the most important question: *Is anyone better off?* How are the students doing? In the lower left quadrant we look first at the number of students who graduated from high school. But what does it mean to say 300 students graduated from high school last year? Does the number 300 tell us anything? Not much. What we really want to know is the percent. Was it 50% or 80%? We could push ourselves a lot harder in education by asking "What percent of 9th graders graduated on time four years later and entered college or employment following graduation?" That would be a

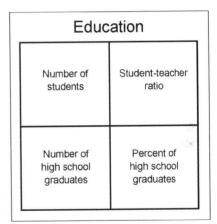

Figure 4.3

tough measure of the effect we have on students' lives. Other education measures in the lower right quadrant include the percent of students with good attendance and the percent of students who are proficient in reading, writing, math and science.

Consider a typical **health plan or practice**. Measures for *How much did we do?* include the number of patients treated, number of appointments and hours of treatment. Measures for *How well did we do it?* include average time in the waiting room, and the retention rates for nursing and clerical staff. *Is anyone better off?* measures in the lower left quadrant include the number of incidents of preventable disease. But the more important measure is the rate of preventable disease, shown in the lower right quadrant. In both cases, these measures are for people in the health plan or practice, not the whole community. The rate of preventable disease in the whole community is Population Accountability. Measures in the lower quadrants also include the number and percent of children in the practice who are fully immunized?[70]

Consider a typical **drug and alcohol treatment program**. Measures for *How much did we do?* include the number of persons treated. Measures for *How well did we do it?* include the percent of staff with advanced training or certification. However, what you really want to know is the number and more importantly the percent of your clients who

Health Plan or Practice

Number of patients treated	Average time in the waiting room
Incidence of preventable disease (in practice)	Rate of preventable disease (in practice)

Figure 4.4

Drug/Alcohol Treatment

Number of persons treated	Percent of staff with training certification
Number of clients off of alcohol & drugs - at exit - 12 months after exit	Percent of clients off of alcohol & drugs - at exit - 12 months after exit

Figure 4.5

are off of alcohol and drugs - at program exit, and 12 months later if you can get that data. This is what is really important, the change in peoples' lives you produce.

The categories work well for programs outside of education, health and social services. Consider a **fire department**. Measures for *How much did we do?* include the number of responses to an alarm. Measures for *How well did we do it?* include the average response time. We know 3 minutes is better than 3 hours. But is anyone better off? Here is a measure that fire departments around the world are using: number and percent of fires kept to the room of origin. This measure applies to the fires where the department was called on to respond. This contrasts with such measures as total fire deaths, injuries or property damage in a geographic catchment area that are population indicators for which a range of partners beyond the fire department share responsibility.

Consider a Department of Transportation's work on **road maintenance**. Measures for *How much did we do?* include the number of miles of road maintained. Measures for *How well did we do it?* include the cost of maintenance per mile and the

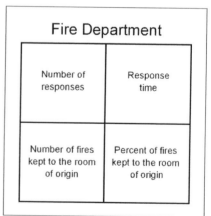

Fire Department

Number of responses	Response time
Number of fires kept to the room of origin	Percent of fires kept to the room of origin

Figure 4.6

---

70. Of course, medical practices, like all businesses have measures in the lower quadrants concerning financial success like profit and return on investment. See the performance measurement examples for General Motors and the discussion of financial measures below.

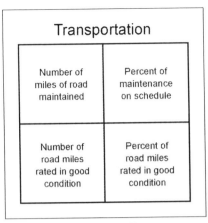

Figure 4.7

percent of maintenance on schedule. However, the bottom line for the customers who ride on those roads are measures like the percent of road miles rated in good condition.[71] This contrasts with highway safety measures, such as rate of fatalities, that are population indicators to which the Department of Transportation contributes.

Consider a Department of Environment's work on **water quality**. Measures for *How much did we do?* include the number of stream sites or stream miles monitored. Measures for *How well did we do it?* include the number of sites monitored per month per worker. But what you really want to know is the effectiveness of the monitoring program as measured by such data as the percent of cited offenders who fully comply with cleanup orders.

These performance measurement categories work for **business** too. Consider the following General Motors examples taken from an article in *USA Today* that featured interviews with the chief executive officers of the biggest US car companies.[72] I went through this article and marked every instance where one of these guys (no gals yet) used data to talk about the performance of his company. Not a single one talked about production hours, or how much steel it took to make a car. One of them talked about a classic efficiency meas-

Water Quality	
Number of stream sites monitored	Average sites monitored per month
Number of cited offenders who fully comply	Percent of cited offenders who fully comply

Figure 4.8

General Motors	
Production hours	Employees per vehicle produced
Number of cars sold	Market share
	Profit per share
Amount of profit	Car value after 2 years

Figure 4.9

ure, employees per vehicle produced, because it took his company more people on average to make a car than his competitors, and he was worried about that. All three talked about some version of the lower right quadrant, market share, profit per share, and car value after two years as a percent of purchase price, because they were concerned with the better-offness of two different groups: stock holders and customers. One of the auto executives went out of his way to point out that the lower left quadrant measure of the number of cars

71. The Department of Transportation in Alaska, for example, uses a 5 part scale to rate the condition of roads.

72. *USAToday*, September 28, 1998.

Baseball

Number of hits	Batting average
Number of games played	Attendance per game
Number of games won	Percent of games won
Number of years in postseason	Percent of years in postseason

Figure 4.10

sold was not very important by itself. What's important, he stated, was profit per share, a lower right quadrant measure.[73]

Just for the fun of it, let's consider **sports**. Baseball is shown in Figure 4.10. You can play a lot of baseball games (*How much did we do?*) and have a high team batting average (*How well did we do it?*). But none of that matters if you don't have a good winning percentage and make postseason play (*Is anyone better off?*). No matter what the sport, it's always the same. Trying hard is not good enough. You have to win.

Notice that there is often a simple mathematical relationship between the quadrants. In the baseball example, the percent of games won (lower right) equals the number of games won (lower left) divided by the number of games played (upper left). In the drug and alcohol treatment example, the percent who quit alcohol and drugs (lower right) equals the number who quit (lower left) divided by the number treated (upper left).

Finally, it is possible to apply these ideas to individual or personal performance. Consider dieting. The number of days on a diet (*How much did we do?*) is not as important as the percent of days on a diet (*How well did we do it?*). And the most important measure is the percent of desired weight loss (*Is anyone better off?*).[74]

There is another important relationship between the quadrants. How well we provide a service (upper right quadrant) has a direct effect on whether, and to what extent, anyone is better off (lower right quadrant). The student teacher ratio

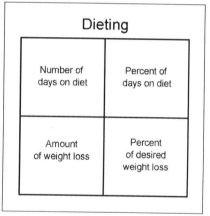

Figure 4.11

has something to do with student achievement. Percent of days on a diet has something to do with percent of desired weight loss. This cause and effect relationship between the upper right and lower right quadrants is one of the most important connections between performance measures. It allows us to pose hypotheses about which aspects of service design and practice produce the best customer results. These hypotheses can be stated in terms of connected upper right and lower right quadrant measures and can be tested using traditional research and evaluation methods. For

73. This is a good illustration of why the lower left quadrant is less important than the lower right quadrant.

74. See "The Little Book of Results-based Dieting" on amazon.com. See also page 141.

this reason, the four quadrants have proved to be a useful tool in the design of evaluation studies.[75]

Finally, there is the well-known tension between quantity and quality. It is possible to produce better customer results by reducing the number of people served. If you spend all your money on just a few customers, your rate of success will almost certainly go up. But other measures will move in the opposite direction. If too much money is spent on too few clients, the unit cost per customer will skyrocket. Conversely, trying to serve too many customers with too few dollars will drive down the *Is anyone better off?* measures. Quantity versus quality is a balancing act for which there is no formula. Choosing the right measures to track can help managers achieve this balance and advocate for the resources they need to deliver high quality services.

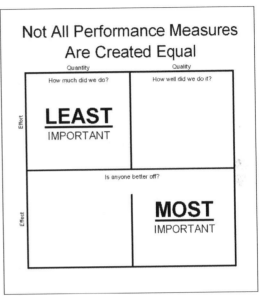

Figure 4.12

Why in the world would you want to sort performance measures into these categories?

Answer: the four quadrants are not equally important. The upper left quadrant, where we count how many people we served and how much activity we performed, is the least important quadrant.[76]

Some people spend their entire careers living in the upper left quadrant counting cases and activity. Somehow we've got to push the discussion to the lower right quadrant measures of whether our customers are better off. And also of great importance is whether we are doing a good job delivering the services we've promised, as measured in the upper right quadrant.

You can think about these quadrants as if they were a physical sorting bin. By sorting measures for your program into these categories you can avoid getting stuck in the upper left quadrant and concentrate on the lower right quadrant measures that tell if your program is working.

---

75. See the discussion of evaluation and how programs contribute to community change in Chapter 7.

76. Not unimportant, just least important.

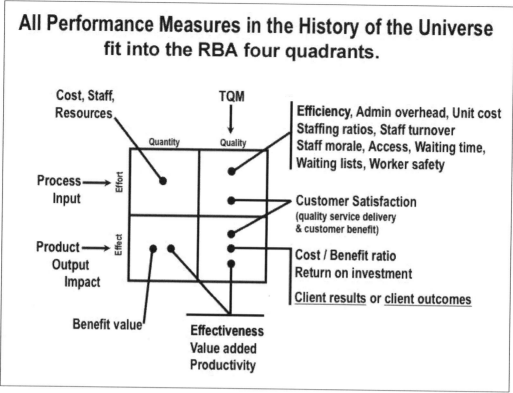

Figure 4.13

Measures for *Is anyone better off?* allow us to address an age-old dilemma in the government and non-profit sectors: the absence of a financial bottom line. Profit is the engine that drives performance improvement in the for-profit sector. Some government programs, like child support enforcement or tax collection, have financial bottom lines. But the vast majority do not. This absence of a bottom line is what makes public and non-profit management so difficult. The answer to this dilemma can be found in the lower right quadrant. ***Is anyone better off? measures are the equivalent of profit for government and non-profit agencies.***

All performance measures in the history of the universe

At the beginning of this chapter, I stated that the three simple categories *How much did we do? How well did we do it?* and *Is anyone better off?* could account for all performance measures in the history of the universe. Here is a chart to back that up.

Most of us grew up with the terms "efficiency" and "effectiveness" as the terms of art in this field. You would think, considering the age and venerability of these two terms that they would account for all performance measures. But they don't.

Efficiency is just one type of performance measure in the upper right quadrant. We want to deliver services efficiently. We sometimes use unit cost or administrative overhead rates to gauge efficiency. But there are many other measures in the upper right quadrant in addition to efficiency including workload ratios, staff turnover rates[77], access, waiting time, customer satisfaction[78] and worker safety. These measures also tell how well service was delivered, in addition to efficiency.

In the lower quadrants, we account for all the terms that have been used to measure effect. Customer satisfaction appears here as well, since customer satisfaction can also tell you if your customers are better off. Other well-known measures in the lower quadrants include: product, impact, benefit value, effectiveness, value added, productivity, cost / benefit ratio, return on investment, and the most important of all performance measures, customer results or customer outcomes. As a shorthand, we will begin referring to the entire set of lower right quadrant measures as "customer results."[79]

Every term in the history of performance measurement seems to fit into one of the quadrants. If this is true, then it means that we can get rid of much of the jargon in this field and begin using three simple, plain language categories to label all performance measures: *How much did we do? How well did we do it? Is anyone better off?* A growing number of public and private sector agencies have adopted these three categories as their official categories for performance measurement.

This chart also helps explain all the convoluted schemes for categorizing performance measures that have emerged over the past 50 years. The problem is created when efficiency and effectiveness are viewed as performance measurement categories **of equal importance**.[80] These schemes then try to fill in the many missing pieces by creating other measurement categories of equal importance. This often leads to the creation of ten or more such categories. The answer, it turns out, is not to create more

---

77. A good way to measure turnover is the percent of employees who have been with you one year or more. If only 10% meet this test, then you are in trouble. If 90% meet this test then you have a pretty stable workforce.

78. Customer satisfaction is discussed in more detail in the next section.

79. Some people correctly point out that customer results should have two components that parallel the difference between results and indicators at the population level, i.e. a plain language statement of client well-being (customers are self sufficient) and a measurement that describes this condition of well-being (% of customers who get jobs). In practice, these two ideas are collapsed into a single term, "customer results." Experience suggests that when these two elements are separated in Performance Accountability, as they must be at the population level, the process loses its common sense feel and becomes unnecessarily complicated. The distinction between a measure's lay definition and technical definition, discussed on page 171, provides for a useful version of this separation.

80. The psychology behind this comes again from the way we talk. The words efficiency and effectiveness are always said together, so they must have equal standing.

categories equal to efficiency, but to identify the category within which efficiency fits, namely *How well did we do it?*. To my knowledge this has not been done before.[81]

Customer satisfaction

Customer satisfaction is one type of measure that applies, without exception, to all services.

There are two kinds of customer satisfaction measures, one in the upper right quadrant and one in the lower right quadrant. Here are two customer satisfaction survey questions that illustrate the difference:

> "Were you treated with respect in the waiting room?" yields a *How well did we do it?* measure.

> "Has your child's behavior improved since we started working with you?" yields an *Is anyone better off?* measure.

A few years ago, I met with the director of a small rural community mental health center and a few of his colleagues. And after just a few minutes of conversation he said to me, "We don't have any data. We can't do this." So I asked him, "Do you think you could take a 10% sample of your customers each month and ask them two questions?"

He thought for a minute. "10%, two questions. Yes, I think we could do that." So, together, we fashioned two questions, one in the upper right quadrant, one in the lower right quadrant. The upper right quadrant question was five words long: (1) **"Did we treat you well?"** This question addresses matters of courtesy, timeliness and cultural competence. The second question was also simple: (2) **"Did we help you with your problems?"** This question addresses whether we made a difference in the customer's life or the life of a family member.

We had created **the world's simplest, and yet complete, customer satisfaction survey**. And he could begin implementing that survey the very next day. This story illustrates another important point. If you, as manager, are not handed the data you need to run your program, you have an obligation to create it. Here was a manager who was willing to create the data he needed while waiting for the perfect computer system to land in his back yard.[82]

Think about how you currently measure customer satisfaction. Most customer satisfaction questionnaires are too long, written at too high a reading level and mix up the two types of customer satisfaction questions as if there's no difference between them.

---

81.   If you think this has been done before, then please send your withering analysis to the Fiscal Policy Studies Institute attention: Withering Analysis Division.

82.   See the more detailed discussion about creating data in Chapter 7.

Try to keep your customer satisfaction surveys short, write the questions in the simplest possible language, and make sure you have covered both types of customer satisfaction questions.

Customer satisfaction surveys can provide three different kinds of useful information. The two questions above provide the basic numbers on whether customer satisfaction is getting better or worse. Then you can ask about the story behind the numbers. Question (3) **"Why did you rate us this way?"** And they can provide specific suggestions. Question (4) **"How can we do better?"** You may be surprised at how many of these suggestions are no-cost or low-cost ideas that can be readily implemented, such as a simple set of guidelines for employees who directly serve customers: 1. Smile and say hello. 2. Call the customer by name. 3. Ask how you can help. 4. Tell them how long they will have to wait. 5. Apologize when things go wrong.[83]

Before we leave the subject, it is important to note that there are special challenges that go with interpreting customer satisfaction data. Response rates are often too low to make the survey data meaningful. Sometimes, customers respond to the survey only when they have a complaint, skewing the survey results toward dissatisfaction. Sometimes customers are afraid that a complaint will get the employee in trouble and give an undeserved positive response, skewing the survey results in the other direction. For these reasons, customer satisfaction data should never be presented without an analysis that helps the reader interpret the data. Customer satisfaction data should also be paired with measures of factual observable customer benefits.

Another problem occurs in the non-competitive public and non-profit sectors, where customers sometimes don't know what a good service is.[84] Customers in a social services office, for example, might think long waits and rude treatment are normal and therefore acceptable. Customers of a drug treatment center might not like the tough program requirements, even though the pro-

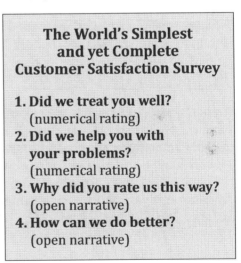

Figure 4.14

---

83. Here's another simple no-cost improvement. Don't you hate it when you are waiting to be served while the employees talk to each other, arrange stock or clean the counter? My father ran a pharmacy for many years and taught me a simple rule. There is **nothing** more important for an employee to do than wait on a customer. Wouldn't it be great if all the businesses you patronize adopted that rule?

84. "Secret shopper" surveys, where people pose as customers and rate the service, are commonly used in the retail industry and provide good approximations of customer satisfaction without these problems.

gram succeeds in getting people off drugs. Parents who know and like the school principal may let that cloud their view of how the school is actually performing for their children. For many programs, customer education may be an important component of an agency's work on customer satisfaction.

Performance measures for administrative services[85]

Administrative services include budget, finance, information systems, human resources, building management, public relations, legal counsel, audit and other functions that provide the infrastructure of an organization. Administrative units routinely count how much they do, such as the number of invoices processed, and how well they do it such as the percent of invoices paid in 30 days. But *Is anyone better off?* measures are often much harder to find.

The primary customers of administrative services are other staff of the organization or "internal customers." It follows that the quality of administrative services can be judged by how well they help internal staff do their jobs. This can sometimes be directly measured. For example, the percent of time the computer system is working properly during peak business hours is a direct measure of how well the information systems division is supporting its users. Such direct measures are relatively rare. This makes measures of customer satisfaction particularly important for administrative services. When you can't think of any other way to determine if your customers are better off, ask them. The most important question to be asked for administrative services is "Are we providing the support you need to do a good job?" Helping other employees succeed is the first and most important purpose of administrative services.[86]

There is another important benefit for administrative services that comes from conducting customer satisfaction surveys. Such surveys, if they are done well and taken seriously, can help build better relationships between the administrative and service delivery staff in the organization. When I worked in government, there was often a wide gulf and sometimes open hostility between these two parts of the department. Organizations work better when administrative and program people get along, and customer satisfaction surveys can help.

Another challenge concerns how to conduct these surveys. In one organization, the administrative units sent out separate questionnaires on different schedules. Man-

---

[85.] For more examples of performance measures for administrative services see Appendix F, and also raguide.org Question 3.11: "How do we identify performance measures for administrative functions?"

[86.] Administrative units typically have two purposes: control and support. Human Resources, for example, enforces the personnel rules but also supports managers in hiring and managing staff. Administrative staff tend to err on the side of control. Those who supervise administrative units need to help staff achieve a balance between these sometimes conflicting roles.

agers complained that they were constantly being asked to fill out surveys, and they didn't take the surveys seriously. Consider doing a single survey covering all administrative areas, so people get only one questionnaire. Or schedule surveys so people know what to expect. This will help get a better response and better information.

The matter of control

Concern about lack of control is the sub-text of all discussions of performance measurement. If people are not talking about this then they are thinking about it. It is the number one excuse why people don't measure performance.

As you go from the upper left quadrant to the lower right quadrant, you have progressively less and less data. It is much easier to get data about how many people you served than it is to get data about whether anyone is better off. But, you also have progressively less and less control over how good you look on that data. The classic example is the recidivism rate for corrections programs, the percent of people who commit another crime after being released from jail or prison. Some corrections officials object to being measured on these rates because the rates have a lot more to do with things that happened outside the facility than anything that happened inside the facility.

These officials are saying, in effect, "I don't control the measure and therefore it's not a valid measure of my program." Have you ever said this? Have you ever thought it privately to yourself? Think of one thing in your personal or professional life that you control 100%. Someone in my workshops once thought he had 100% control of his pet goldfish. But I had little kids, and we had goldfish. We woke up one morning to find the fish belly up in the tank. The truth is that there is nothing in our lives that we control 100%. If control is the over-riding criteria for performance measures, then there are no performance measures. Congratulations. You're off the hook.

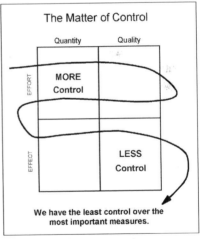

Figure 4.15

Somehow we've got to get used to this paradox: As we go from the least important measures (upper left quadrant) to the most important measures (lower right quadrant), we go from having the most control to having the least control. This is another reason why people spend their whole careers in the upper left quadrant. Fear, pure and simple. It can be scary to look at whether anyone is better off. But then you ask people, "Why did you go into this profession in the first place? Why did you become a teacher, a social worker, a public health nurse, a police officer?" The answers are all in the lower right quadrant. They wanted to make peoples' lives better. Yet often all we measure is how many people we served?

Funders can be part of this problem. When you fill out your monthly or quarterly report back to your funders, they always ask for the number of people served. Funders often don't know how to ask if customers are better off. If you are good at answering this question, you will be much more successful at fund raising because people give you money to make a difference in your customers' lives.

What is the response to the "lack of control" objection? Simple. **Get over it.** No one controls all the factors that affect their performance. Performance in the supposedly clearer environment of business is just as complicated. Business sales are affected by many factors, including demographic changes, market forces and weather, to name a few. A salesperson who complained that they shouldn't be held accountable for sales because of these outside forces would be promptly fired.

Think of all the factors that affect whether your customers are better off. Do you control these factors? Of course not. Should you still be accountable for whether your customers are better off? Definitely yes.

Summary of performance measures

The following chart provides a summary of the various types of measures found in each quadrant. It will be helpful to have this chart handy when choosing performance measures for your program or agency.

How much did we do?	How well did we do it?
# Customers served (by customer characteristic)	% Common measures — Workload ratio, staff turnover rate, staff morale, percent of staff fully trained, worker safety, unit cost, customer satisfaction: *Did we treat you well?*
# Activities (by type of activity)	% Activity-specific measures — Percent of actions timely and correct, percent clients completing activity, percent of actions meeting standards

Is Anyone Better Off?	
# Skills / Knowledge	% Skills / Knowledge
# Attitude / Opinion	% Attitude / Opinion including customer satisfaction: *Did we help you with your problems?*
# Behavior	% Behavior
# Circumstance	% Circumstance

Figure 4.16

The upper left quadrant measures typically include the number of customers and activities. These can be broken out by customer characteristic or type of activity.

The upper right quadrant measures include a set of Common Measures that apply to many different programs, such as turnover rate and unit cost. There are also "Activity Specific" measures in this quadrant. For each activity in the upper left quadrant, there are one or more measures in the upper right quadrant that tell how well that particular activity is performed. For example, if the activity is the number of telephone calls answered, then the activity specific measure might be the percent answered on the 1st or 2nd ring. If the activity is the number of hospital discharge plans produced, then the activity specific measure might be the percent produced on time and with family participation.

The lower quadrant measures almost always come in pairs of number and percentage. For example, the number and percent who graduated high school or the number and percent who got off of alcohol and drugs. The lower quadrant measures almost always have to do with one of four dimensions of better-offness: skills / knowledge, attitude / opinion, behavior and circumstance. Think of these categories as rocks to look under when trying to find performance measures.

Skills and knowledge measures include achievement test scores for students, and percent of participants in parent training who show improved skills.

Attitude and opinion measures include percent of students with high personal ambitions and percent of customers who believe the service helped them with their problems.

Behavior measures include percent of students with good school attendance and percent of public housing residents who pay their rent on time.

Circumstance (or condition) measures include percent of customers who are employed in jobs above the minimum wage, percent of customers in stable housing and percent of road-miles in good condition

All programs have multiple measures in the lower right quadrant. Some of these measures will be more important than others. Try to identify as many measures as possible before winnowing them down to the most important measures. The method described in Appendix G can help you identify measures and winnow them down to the 3 to 5 most important headline measures and a Data Development Agenda.

Using performance measures to improve performance: the 7 Questions

Now that we have established the three types of performance measures, we are ready to address the talk to action thinking process for Performance Accountability. This is very similar to the population process presented in Chapter 3, with two important differences. Performance Accountability begins with the program's customers, while Population Accountability begins with a population in a geographic area. And the method used to identify performance measures is different from the method used to establish results and indicators.

The full Performance Accountability talk to action thinking process is shown as a schematic in Figure 4.17 and in the form of 7 Questions in Figure 4.18. The 4-Quadrant method for identifying performance measures, presented in Appendix G, can help you get a beginning set of answers to questions 1, 2 and 3 and a head start on question 4.

1. Who are our customers? Customers are the people whose lives are affected, for better or worse, by the actions of the program. Most programs have more than one customer group, and sometimes these customer groups have competing or even conflicting interests. My favorite example of this comes from the Alaska Fish and Game Commission where their customers include the fishermen and the fish. You will never find two customer groups with less in common. They resolved this conflict by choosing "sustainable yield" as one of their most important lower right quadrant measures, a measure that showed how well they balanced the competing interests of their different customer groups.

I encountered another interesting debate about customers in a state department of education. One group of staff argued that the state department had no direct contact with students and therefore the customers must be the superintendents, principals and teachers with whom they worked. A second group of staff argued that the principle purpose of the department was student achievement and therefore the department's customers must be the students. The correct answer is both. The lives of both students and teachers are affected by the actions of the department of education. The issue was settled by calling superintendents, principals, and teachers direct customers and students indirect customers.

Your program or agency will also have multiple customer groups and you need to develop a complete list of who these groups are. If it is helpful you can distinguish between direct and indirect customers, primary and secondary customers, or internal and external customers.

There are several other important ways in which customers can be defined. There are times when organizations are customers. A United Way providing support to its grantees can consider the grantee organizations themselves as customers. This allows us to look at lower right quadrant measures about the behavior or achievement of these organizations. For example, the percentage of organizations that are in good financial condition or the percentage that have identified and are using performance measures in a continuous improvement process.

For services that build and maintain infrastructure, such as departments of transportation or water and sewer divisions, the roads, bridges and pipelines can be treated as customers for purposes of identifying performance measures. This allows us to assess the performance of these organizations based on the condition of the infrastructure system components. For example the percentage of roads and bridges rated in good condition, or the rate of water main breaks.

2. How can we measure if our customers are better off? These are the lower right quadrant *Is anyone better off?* measures. If your program does a really good job, how are your customers' lives better? Conversely, if you did a really bad job, how would their lives be worse? Think about the most meaningful measures, whether you have data or not. Remember not to exclude measures because you don't fully control performance. Measures in this category will <u>always</u> be those for which you have the least control.

3. How can we measure if we're delivering services well? These are the upper right quadrant measures that tell if the program's activities are performed well. These measures are usually about what staff do, and how well the functions of the program are performed. Think about the most meaningful measures whether you have data or not.

4. How are we doing on the most important of these measures? There are two parts to this question. From the measures identified in questions 2 and 3 about customers and service delivery, what are the 3 to 5 most important headline measures. Try to get a healthy mix of measures from each category.

For each of these measures, create a baseline that shows the history of performance and a forecast of where you are heading if you don't do anything more or different. If the data is not handy, then make your best guess about what this graph would look like. Tell the story behind this picture. Why are things getting better or worse? What are the causes and forces at work that explain the picture of your performance? Take credit for what's working and be honest about what's not working.

Identify where you need new and better data and create a Data Development Agenda. Identify questions you need answered in order to fully understand the story behind the baseline. Put these questions into an Information and Research Agenda about causes.

5. Who are the partners who have a role to play in doing better? Consider partners inside and outside the organization who might be able to help improve performance. Push beyond the usual suspects. Think about long-shots here. Make sure you include young people, parents and other customers. It is sometimes useful to distinguish between active and non-active partners, so that you can work to engage the non-active partners as part of your action plan.

6. What works to do better, including no-cost and low-cost ideas? There are two natural pointers to what works. Each cause points to actions you could take to address that cause, and each partner has something to contribute. Consider what the research says about what works. Be creative and think of non-conventional solutions. Insist that people think about no-cost low-cost actions. If you need more information about what works, make these questions Part 2 of your Information and Research Agenda.

7. What do we propose to do? This is the most important question. It is the action part of getting from talk to action. You can use the criteria *specificity, leverage, values and reach* (see page 44) to choose the most powerful actions from the possibilities identified in question 6 about what could work to do better. Organize these actions into a plan that specifies the person responsible for each task, the start and end dates and necessary resources.

These questions are designed to be answered quickly and then repeated. It is possible to take a pass at all 7 questions in anywhere from 20 minutes to an hour.

Use the 7 Questions in every supervisory relationship

The 7 questions should be asked and answered on a regular basis in every supervisory relationship throughout the system. A supervisor should have regular conferences with subordinates. Imagine that you handed out the 7 Questions a few days before your next supervisory conference. You say, "We're going to take the first 15 minutes of our time together to talk about your best answers to these questions. I don't expect you to get it perfect. Just take a crack at it. Then we're going to have that discussion every time we get together for the rest of your life." If you were to do this, you would begin to change the culture of your organization.

Performance Accountability is about culture change. One of the things we've learned from Chaos and Complexity Theory is that culture change doesn't happen in complex organizations through big events, like one or two training sessions. Culture change happens with little events that happen thousands of times in the life of an organization. Asking and answering the 7 Questions at every intersection of supervision is a little event that could happen thousands of times in the life of your organization (from the executive to the front line) that would profoundly change how people think about customers (Question 1), how they think about data (Questions 2,3, and 4) and how they think about using data to improve performance (Questions 5, 6, and 7).

The idea of using the 7 Questions in every supervisory relationship is important for another reason. It means that each supervisory relationship is the unit of change for implementing Performance Accountability. If there are 100 supervisory relationships in the organization, then each relationship represents 1% of full implementation.

Using the 7 questions is not rocket science. Managers and supervisors can be trained to do this quickly and will get good at it through practice. This presents a large number of options regarding how to phase in Performance Accountability. It is not necessary to direct everyone to use the 7 questions all at once. It is not necessary to run huge training sessions and hire lots of consultants to hold supervisors' hands. Nor is it necessary to institute a new burdensome regimen of forms to be filled out. **You can simply start using this method, right now, one supervisor at a time.**

Get to the point planning

Notice that the 7 Questions skip past mission, vision, values, purpose, problems, issues, goals, objectives, needs assessments and environmental scans and go directly to performance measures. This goes against the orthodoxy of the planning profession which dictates that some combination of these other processes must be completed before getting to measurement. Baloney.

Many people seem to think that the agency's mission statement must be perfected before anything else can be done. I have seen this process take six months or more. It may be a good idea for an agency to have a mission statement, but it is unnecessarily time consuming and burdensome to try to develop performance measures from these statements. Unless you are thinking of creating a brand new agency, most programs have established purposes and can begin using performance measures immediately.

Think about it this way. Programs are created through a population level decision process that determines whether the program should **exist or not**. Performance Accountability picks up at this point, takes the program's existence as a given, and moves to the next step of answering whether it's **working or not**. In this construct, it can be argued that **mission statements are by-products of selecting performance measures**, not the other way around. After the most important lower right quadrant performance measures are identified, they can be used to help craft a mission statement. For example, staff in a job training program will readily identify the following two performance measures: the percent of people placed in good paying jobs, and the percent who keep those jobs at least six months. This could then help them craft the following mission statement: "Our mission is to help people get and keep good paying jobs."

Traditional planning systems waste an inordinate amount of time before people are allowed to talk about performance measures. By going straight to the business of selecting performance measures, we ease the frustration and cynicism that goes with complex planning processes. We go directly to the heart of Performance Accountability, **the disciplined use of data in day-to-day management.**

Monthly or quarterly review of performance

Managers should review performance on a monthly or quarterly basis in staff meetings and individual supervisory conferences. There should be three or four charts on the wall for the most important measures. In supervisory conferences, the charts should be on a single piece of paper.

The agenda should track the seven Performance Accountability questions:

1. Customers: Start each meeting by remembering who the customers are. It's amazing how quickly this can get confused or forgotten. The list of customers could also be a chart on the wall.

2 and 3. Choice of measures: How can we measure if our customers are better off? How can we measure if we're delivering service well? Revisit your previous answers to these questions. Consider the status of your Data Development Agenda here. Choice of measures is very important in the early stages of doing this work and can be addressed less frequently as the work proceeds.

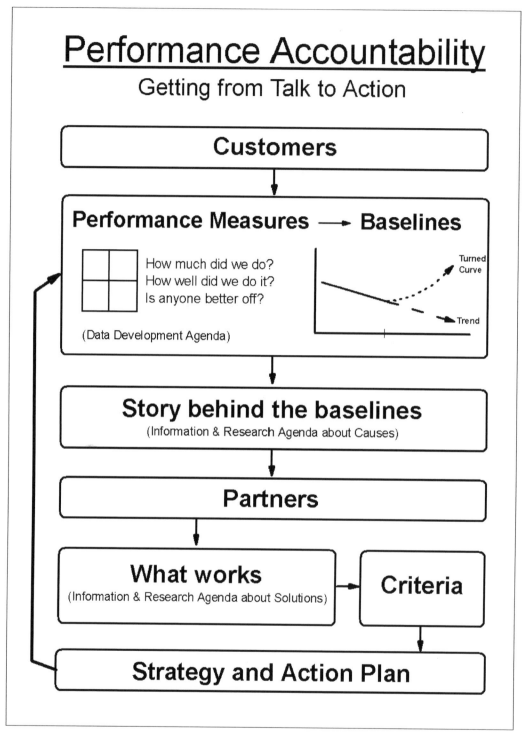

Figure 4.17

The 7 Performance Accountability Questions

1. Who are our customers?

2. How can we measure if our customers are better off?

3. How can we measure if we are delivering services well ?

4. How are we doing on the most important of these measures?

5. Who are the partners that have a role to play in doing better?

6. What works to do better, including no-cost and low-cost ideas?

7. What do we propose to do?

Figure 4.18

4. Current performance: Evaluate performance on the most important measures. Discuss the story behind current performance and progress since the last meeting. Do not go around the room and have everyone report on what they did since the last meeting. Instead use this time for a diagnostic discussion. You have to understand what is causing current performance before you can do better.

5. Partners: Evaluate how successful you have been in engaging new partners and what they contribute. Identify partners that need to be recruited or engaged.

6. What works to do better: Consider what could work to do better. Be creative about possibilities. Make sure you consider no-cost and low-cost actions. Encourage people to suggest "off the wall" ideas.

7. Action plan: Decide what you will do before the next meeting to improve performance. Regarding written monthly or quarterly performance reports - keep them very short, one page of bullet points, or don't do them at all. In all of this work, form should follow function. **Don't create paper if you don't need it.** It's OK to simply keep notes on what people agreed to do. Try these methods without any paper for a while and then decide what form of written material would be useful. Remember one of the cardinal rules of good management: IF IT'S NOT USEFUL, DON'T DO IT.

Comparing performance

There are three ways to compare performance: **to yourself, to others and to standards**. The first and most important comparison is to yourself, using baselines that show the history and forecast of your performance.

Comparing to yourself is a common sense approach that is used all the time in the business world. If we were attending the annual sales meeting of a corporation there would be a baseline chart at the front of the room. It would show the history of sales and where sales were heading if we just continued our current growth rate. The company president would push all of us to do better than the baseline in the coming months.

Child support collections are known to increase in proportion to the growth in the population and the growth in wages. It is possible to forecast the extent to which these forces will drive up collections. Let's say that this forecasted increase is 2% for the next year. If the manager of the child support enforcement program achieves a 2% increase in collections next year, that manager has not actually improved the program's performance. The manager must do better than 2% to show real performance improvement.

All managers should have these kind of baseline charts on their walls or in their desk drawers. When I worked for the state of Maryland, the State Budget Secretary, Lou Stettler, had 15 of these charts arrayed around his office. He could look up at any time and see the baselines for the most important measures of the state's fiscal health.

Comparing to others: When you compare the performance of a group of programs providing the same service, you usually get the majority of programs clustered in the mid range of performance, with a few performing much better and a few performing much worse. What happens when you reward the high performers and punish the low performers? Before you answer this question, you have to know **why** one group is doing well and the other group is doing poorly.

The high performing group may be doing well because they have all the easy cases and the low performing group may have all the tough cases. If you reward one and punish the other, you send a simple message throughout the service system: "Skim the easy cases for yourself. Dump the tough cases on someone else." We see examples of this skimming all the time. There was a managed health care provider in Florida that was enrolling elders in their health care plan. They put their enrollment office on the third floor and made sure the elevator was always broken. If you could walk up three flights of stairs they wanted you in their plan. It was a brilliant scheme to skim the elder population for people healthy enough to walk up three flights of stairs. Illegal but brilliant.

Comparing to standards: Finally we can compare to standards. There are many well-established standards for how well service is delivered. We have standards for processing applications in 30 days. We have standards for staffing ratios in child care centers and nursing homes. We have standards for handicapped accessibility. There are many useful standards about how service is delivered because there are clear cases where we know what good service looks like.

Standards for measures of whether customers are better off are much more difficult to establish. It's the same problem we encounter when comparing programs to each other. The mixture of easy and hard cases makes it difficult to determine a fair standard for all providers. If you have 15 different welfare to work providers all with different proportions of easy and hard cases, it is not fair to set a single standard (e.g. 70% placement in jobs) for all of them. It will be easy for some to meet this standard and impossible for others. The concept of turning the curve is a much better way to gauge progress on lower right quadrant measures than whether that program has met a fixed standard.

When standards are used to stretch organizations toward higher performance, this should never be done without also using baselines to give credit for incremental improvement. Failing to do this can lead to dysfunctional behavior. A hospital was being judged against standards for in-patient death rates by type of operation. They figured out how to beat the system. If a patient was about to die, they were discharged so it wouldn't show up on their statistics. This hospital looked great on inpatient death rates. It's not a hospital you would want to go to.[87]

---

87. This story is cited in Governing Magazine/May 1998 management column entitled "Poisoned Measures." The magazine admits that it may be apocryphal.

This illustrates another important point. If you manage your program using only one measure, you can look good on that measure at the expense of something else. Maybe the hospital should have tracked a second measure about the well-being of patients 6 weeks after discharge. If the discharged patients were all dead, this would hint at a problem. The hospital's goal should have been to optimize performance simultaneously on in-patient death rates **and** post-discharge recovery.

The danger of perverse incentives can be found in just about any system. If you're a high school principal and want to improve the school's attendance rate, then kick out all the troublemakers. The attendance rate will go up. If you are a social services director and want to bring down foster care caseloads, slow down child abuse investigations. The foster care caseload will begin to decline.

We are not trying to find one magic measure for a program, but rather a **balanced set of three to five measures** taken from *How well did we do it?* and *Is anyone better off?* These can be used to give a "checks and balances" view of program performance. Managers can work toward improving performance on all of them simultaneously.

Using baselines to set targets without creating fear of punishment

When people hear the words "performance measurement" it triggers an association with all the bad things that have ever happened to them since childhood. In almost everyone's experience, the matter of measurement has been connected at one time or another to punishment. This goes back to our earliest memories of school grades and continues right into the workplace. It is no wonder that there is an atmosphere of fear surrounding this work.

Setting targets has been especially problematic. There is a long history of setting unrealistic performance targets and then beating people up when they fail to meet them. This practice is based on the misguided belief that such targets coupled with fear of punishment will lead to better performance. In practice, unrealistic targets detract from credibility. And fear turns out to be one of the worst ways for managers to motivate people. People working within this punishment culture will try to pick measures they look good on or set targets they can easily meet. The measures are rarely the most important ones and the targets are meaningless. The organization appears to be practicing Performance Accountability, but it's a waste of time. There is a better way.

We must first acknowledge that getting people to use data to improve performance is a culture change. Disciplined use of data is a new experience for many managers. In developing a Performance Accountability system, data should first be used in private consultations between employees and their supervisors. This can provide an incubation period, where managers get familiar with how to interpret data and use data to improve performance.[88]

---

[88]   See the discussion of "Inside story - outside story" below.

Performance Accountability should be part of a larger organizational development effort to create a healthy workplace. You can have the best designed accountability system in the world and it will not work in a sick environment. The purpose of Performance Accountability must be improved performance. Recognition should be provided for improved performance as well as outstanding performance.

Another way to avoid the punishment culture is to set targets in a fair and useful way. A target is a specific desired future level of achievement for an indicator or performance measure. Targets are sometimes time specific and sometimes not, "The target is a 95% graduation rate," or "The target is a 95% graduation rate by 2020." A standard is a type of target that has an established relationship to quality service or quality of life conditions. Standards can be minimum acceptable standards such as "no more than 24 hours to respond to a report of child abuse," or high standards to strive for such as "all invoices paid on time."

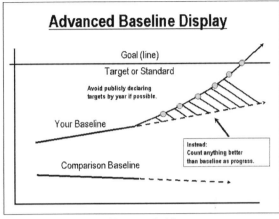

Figure 4.19

The key to effective use of targets is a sense of fair play. Targets should always be set in relation to a baseline. When a date is set for achieving the target, it should look reasonable when viewed against the baseline history and forecast. There is nothing wrong with ambitious targets provided that they are achievable, and there is a method for recognizing incremental progress short of the target. The concept of turning the curve is such a method.

The schematic in Figure 4.19 shows a way to present the three types of comparisons (to yourself, to others and to standards) on the same graph. The performance baseline is presented with history and forecast. A comparison baseline is shown for a similar program. And a goal, target or standard is shown as a horizontal line. The idea is to turn the curve and literally cross the goal line as soon as possible. Anything better than baseline counts as progress.

This stands in contrast to the way we often set targets. We set a 5 year target and then declare year by year exactly where we are going to be along the pathway of improvement. The problem is that you can do a great job of turning the curve, but fall just a little short of where you said you were going to be, and you're a failure. In a small town in Australia, the newly assigned police officer promised a 50% reduction in crime in the first year. He only achieved a 43% reduction. The headlines were "Failed to meet target."

I recommend that you avoid **publicly** declaring **year by year** targets if possible. The only exceptions are when minimum standards of health and safety are involved. Year by year targets or month by month targets can be useful **internally** to motivate and stretch employee performance. But once you declare them publicly, you risk setting yourself up for failure.

This baseline format should become the standard way in which you present all of your most important data, whether your funders ask for it or not. Fill out all the forms that the funder requires, but provide this presentation as well. It allows you to claim credit for progress even if you do not reach some predetermined target. And it allows you to challenge targets that are unreasonable or unfair.

One of the best examples of this format is Healthy People 2010, published by the US Department of Health and Human Services. For each of the health indicators presented in this document, an historical baseline is presented, and a horizontal line is drawn representing the national goal for that indicator for 2010. It is easy to see if the nation is making progress toward this goal, and judge the chances of achieving it at the current pace of change.

Inside story - Outside story

Closely related to the matter of setting targets is the matter of how and when organizational performance is thrust into the public view. This is not always a matter of choice. School performance data is now routinely published in the newspapers whether the schools are ready for it or not. And performance that concerns unethical or illegal behavior should never be withheld or hidden. But, no one wants to look bad in public, and Performance Accountability systems sometimes fail because they raise the stakes too high and too fast.

Programs and agencies need to understand their performance and have a plan to fix it before they explain it publicly. While embarrassment is sometimes unavoidable, you cannot ask managers to support a system that **deliberately** embarrasses them.

Managers will sometimes need to have an "inside story" and an "outside story." The inside story must be the unadulterated truth, a straight look in the mirror about how well the program or agency is performing. When managers understand the truth about their performance, they can figure out what to do about it and how to tell their performance story to the outside world.

The problem arises when the only story a program or agency has is its "outside" story. This means that the manager and senior staff don't even know the truth about their own performance. **They are not just lying to the outside world, they are lying to themselves.** If Performance Accountability is going to work, then complete truthfulness is the only way.

We should require managers to have a completely truthful inside story, and then help them figure out how to tell that story to the outside world. This suggests a way of telling the outside story that is powerful and compelling and yet is rarely used. In a public setting with elected officials, stakeholders, or constituents, the presentation goes like this:

> *"Here's where we are doing well.*
> *Here's where we are not doing as well as we would like, and*
> *Here's what we are doing to get better."*

A good offense is the best defense. Give them the good news first. Take credit for what you have accomplished. Then give them the bad news before they force it out of you. Then tell them what you plan to do to get better. You might even ask for their help in funding the necessary improvements.

This is scary and somewhat risky. But this approach gets you two things. It gets you credit for what you're doing well. More importantly it gets you **credibility** for telling the truth even when it's difficult. And credibility is the single most precious commodity in management and politics.

Is my program working?

Did you skip ahead to this section? Do you have an urgent presentation to make? If the first purpose of Performance Accountability is to improve performance, then the next purpose is to demonstrate that the program is working.

The question of whether a program is working has two parts. The first part is about process and the second part is about customer results.

Process: Let's take the easier process questions first. "Is my program doing what it's supposed to do?" and "Is the program doing it well?" Most programs are designed to provide certain services in a certain way. Process evaluations can test if the program is operating true to its design. In a treatment program, for example, it is possible to determine if the treatment regimen in practice conforms to the program's design. In a school, it is possible to determine if teachers are in fact teaching the prescribed curriculum.

The next question is whether the program's prescribed functions are being performed well. Here we can use the *How well did we do it?* measures to determine if the functions are timely, accurate and properly staffed. What percent of applications are processed on time? What percent of staff have completed relevant training? Are staff workload ratios within an acceptable range? Problems related to program design most often require changes in policy such the hours the treatment clinic is open. Problems with program implementation most often require changes in practice such as hiring more staff.

Results: The second part of "Is my program working?" is about customer results. This is a much more important and much more difficult question to answer. "Are our customers' lives getting better?" and "To what extent did the program cause this change?" What is the high school graduation rate? What percent of 3rd graders can read at grade level? Are job training graduates getting good paying jobs? We can test how we're doing on these measures and determine whether performance is getting better or worse.

There is an underlying question that is always present when considering customer results. Did my program **cause** the customer's improvement? This is the **most** difficult question to answer. There are a few reasonably straightforward methods that can be used to demonstrate that a program has had a positive effect on its customers. But any attempt to discern the extent to which the program caused this improvement runs up against profound questions about the very nature of causality in complex environments. We'll give four straightforward methods in this section. The nature of causality in complex environments will be a completely and definitively addressed in chapter 7.[89]

1. Control group research: is the "gold standard"[90] for demonstrating cause and effect. Create two groups with comparable characteristics. Provide treatment to one. Deny treatment to the other. See if there's any difference in the customer, student or patient results. These methods are used all the time in medical research. The principal problems that go with control group research are expense and ethics. Control group research is very expensive. Most programs can't afford to do it. There are also legal and ethical restrictions in human research about withholding treatment that is believed to work.

There are some rare circumstances where control groups occur naturally and it is possible to create comparisons with relatively little effort and expense. When Pennsylvania implemented its first family preservation programs, there were not enough slots for all the families who qualified for the service, and a waiting list was created. Since families were not triaged from this list, the families waiting for service were very much like the families receiving service. An analysis showed that there were higher rates of foster care entry from the waiting list families than the families in the program. This suggested that the family preservation program was making a difference on the rate of entry into foster care. Using this data, it was possible to estimate the program's effect on foster care caseload and cost. Such comparisons can also occur between jurisdictions where some jurisdictions adopt a policy and others don't. States with motorcycle helmet laws, for example, show lower accident related medical and rehabilitation costs than those without.

2. Direct measurement: Another way to determine program contribution to customer change is by selecting performance measures that directly compare the customer's condition at two points in time. For example, a tutoring program could compare a student's grades at the beginning of the program with grades later in the school year. Any significant pattern of improvement would represent evidence of program contribution to the change.

---

89.   See "Demonstrating program contribution to community change." in Chapter 7.
90.   So called because it costs a lot of gold.

3. Comparisons to similar programs or populations: Other kinds of performance measurement comparisons can also help quantify the extent of program contribution to customer change. You can compare your performance to that of a similar program whose effect on customers has been formally tested. If your program's success rates fall near those of the comparable program, you can piggyback on their documentation to demonstrate your program's effect.

Still another comparison looks at your customers' results compared to relevant population characteristics in the areas from which your customers are drawn. If, for example, the rate of repeat teen pregnancy for the young women in your program is lower than the rate for other teens in their neighborhoods, you can argue that the program contributed to this difference.

These kinds of comparisons are among the most commonly used, but they are replete with difficulties. No two programs are ever exactly the same. Programs with the same names and designs still operate differently and serve different customers. The same problem applies to comparisons with neighborhood population characteristics. The case for comparability between programs or neighborhood populations must be compelling or at least credible to make these methods believable and useful.

4. Customer opinion: Finally, when all else fails, ask the customers if the service made a difference. "Did this training help you become a better teacher?" "Did these counseling sessions help improve your child's behavior at home and at school?" Like all customer satisfaction surveys, the data can be difficult to interpret and may be viewed with suspicion. People in positions of authority tend not to believe self reporting of benefits. But customers are the ultimate judge of a program's success and their opinions, compiled as data or given as stories, can be useful evidence that the program is working.

The performance of service systems

A service system is a set of programs or agencies with common customers and related purposes. The education service system includes pre-school child care, primary and secondary education, adult education programs, and colleges and universities. The health care system includes public and private sector doctors, hospitals, clinics, rehabilitation services, long term care, and support services like laboratories and ambulances. The out of home care system for children includes public child welfare services, juvenile justice, and mental health services, and residential and therapeutic providers supporting children in care. Subsets of these service systems can also constitute a service system. For example, the higher education system is often considered separately from the education system as a whole.

Performance measures can be developed for service systems. The most important measures can usually be derived by adding together comparable measures from the systems' component parts. In health care, it is possible to calculate a rate of emergency room usage for the system as a whole by adding together the usage data for individual hospitals. In higher education, the percent of freshman who reach graduation can be calculated by adding together the data for individual institutions.

There are some measures, however, that are only meaningful at the system level where more than one agency is involved. These include such measures as the average number of case workers assigned to the same family, or the average number of different offices that clients must visit each month to get the services they need. These kind of systemic measures cannot be produced by adding agency data but must be separately gathered across the system, usually on a sample basis.

These kind of cross-system measures give an operational definition to otherwise vague notions like coordinating services or service integration. If services are truly coordinated, then customers should have fewer case managers to deal with and fewer offices to visit. Managers of a service system can join together to use these measures to consider the system performance as a whole, and work to improve that performance.

But we already have so many reporting requirements imposed on us

Yes, everyone does. You spend so much time filling out forms for other people that you have no performance system for yourself at all. The sum total of your funders' reporting requirements should not be your performance system. Instead, you should create a performance system that makes sense to you and your staff, and it should actually be **useful** in running the program.

If you do this well, it will provide most of the information you need to meet your funders' reporting requirements. Meeting these requirements will become a **byproduct** of your system. Furthermore, you will be more successful with funders because your program performs better. Think about using this approach when designing the management information systems for your organization. Put your management needs first and allow the funders' forms to follow.[91]

How to implement Performance Accountability

The history of performance measurement goes like this: One morning the chief executive comes charging out of the shower all fired up about performance measurement, gets to the office, declares that starting tomorrow every unit of the agency will have performance measures. Three months later, the organization has generated a thousand pages of paper, most of it completely useless. Eventually the system collapses under its own weight until, several years later, the next executive comes charging out of the shower. This is the life cycle of performance measurement systems. Trying to implement Performance Accountability on a grand scale in a single stroke is almost always a mistake. Implementing Performance Accountability should proceed in stages and is best done both top down and bottom up.

[91.] Another case of forms following function.

Let's start with the **bottom up**. Find the three or four best managers in your organization at the operational level. Provide support for these people in the form of a coach or mentor. Help them identify performance measures and use the 7 Questions on a regular basis. Don't prescribe forms and reports at first. Let them play with and adapt the process and see what forms emerge. Consider this an experiment where the purpose is to make the products useful to the manager. Post the most important performance baselines on the wall. When these people have a good story to tell, allow them to showcase their work using presentation methods that track the 7 Questions. (See the Turn the Curve report format Appendix E.) In other words, help them be successful.

Once you have examples of success, then grow the work up through the organization. The managers who do the best work can become coaches for those who come later. For those of your staff who are resistant or just don't get it, assign a coach, send them to training or send them to a desert island. Let people see that performance measures actually get used. Give the success stories to your public relations staff to use in newsletters and press releases.

Equally important is the work from the **top down**. If people in the organization are going to take the work seriously, then senior staff must model this behavior. The agency director should ask each of the people reporting directly to her or him to bring their best answers to the 7 Questions to their next one-on-one conference. In the first few meetings, focus on getting the right performance measures and establishing baselines. After this, focus on the questions about the story behind the baselines and what will be done to get better.

Make this discussion the **first** 15 minutes of every meeting, not something you get to if you have time. After a few sessions, the performance measures could become the basis for a short performance report that is used for setting organizational or personal goals. As senior managers prepare for their meeting with the boss, they will find they need to ask the same questions of the people who report to them. This begins the process of building down through the organization. After a few months, the second tier of managers can be required to use this same process with their staff.

This process will lead to consensus about what measures are most important for the organization and allow baselines for these measures to be updated on a regular basis. A few of these baselines should be posted on the wall in the conference room where staff meetings are held. Some might be permanently on display. Others might rotate through the different component parts of the organization. At the monthly staff meetings, staff can take turns making short 15-minute presentations about what they do by answering the 7 Questions and making reference to their baseline performance charts.

This approach sends two very important messages. First, performance measurement is taken seriously by management, and top managers are willing to practice what they preach. Secondly, and perhaps more importantly, performance measurement is part of day-to-day management, not a back-burner exercise.

Begin using the performance measures and analysis in the organization's internal budget deliberations. Using performance measures in the budget process makes another statement about its importance. Use the 7 Questions to structure internal budget deliberations. Keep it simple.[92] Don't let the budget process add unnecessary complexity to the forms or process and don't let it become the primary reason for doing this work.

If you are a mid-level manager and work in an organization where you are the only one who seems to understand this approach, try it quietly for your part of the organization. Become an island of excellence. Take credit for the improvements in performance you are able to achieve. Begin presenting your work to others using RBA Performance Accountability methods. When top management notices, **and they will**, help them understand how this could be used more broadly in the organization.

---

[92]   Most people don't know the second half of "Keep it simple, stupid." (KISS). It's "Or face failure." (OFF).

WHERE RESULTS-BASED ACCOUNTABILITY THINKING HAS WORKED

North Lincolnshire Council, United Kingdom[93]

The North Lincolnshire Council has responsibility for a wide range of public services for a population of approximately 150,000. One of those services is public housing. The Council directly owns and manages over 10,000 housing units, approximately 15% of the area's housing stock.

In 2001, the national Housing Inspectorate reviewed the North Lincolnshire public sector housing services and rated it as a "poor service." In 2003, the inspectors returned and found that the service had actually gotten worse. The housing service was near the bottom of virtually all of the national performance tables. In 2000, over 3.5% of the stock was empty, compared with the top performing authorities that had a vacancy rate of only 0.75%. The inspectors were so concerned about the overall state of the service that they threatened to take the service out of local control unless the Council could produce a convincing recovery plan.

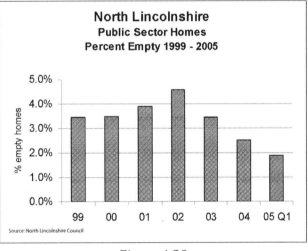

Figure 4.20

These findings were disappointing and embarrassing for the Council. Since the creation of the North Lincolnshire Council in 1996, elected members, managers and staff had worked hard to develop high-quality services. Some of the Council's services, notably social care services and educational services, were judged to be among the best in the country. In the weeks that followed the re-inspection, the social and housing department put together a Recovery and Continuous Improvement Plan. The purpose of this plan was to raise service performance to high levels and develop a capacity for self improvement that would carry the service beyond the life of the plan.

---

93.   Thanks to Nigel Richardson, Executive Director, Social and Housing Services and Mike Pinnock Head of Learning, Development and Support, and their colleagues at the North Lincolnshire Council.

Think outcomes: The newly appointed head of social and housing services, and one of his senior staff, drew on previous experience using Outcomes Based Accountability (OBA) in social care services. The new plan involved 16 tracks of improvement work. One of these was an effort to improve the turnaround of empty properties and make them ready for re-occupancy. Managers within the service had traditionally called these empty properties "voids." The director insisted that staff start talking about "empty homes" to link the effort to the wider community outcome of helping people create decent and affordable homes.

Process makes perfect: A team of staff and tenants completely revamped the process of preparing vacant properties for re-letting to assure quality and also reduce turn-around times. They began classifying all properties according to the amount of work needed, creating a fast track for properties that required minimal work. Each property was assessed against a set of quality standards by tenant inspectors. Two tenant "champions" were nominated to lead the implementation of the work.

If you can't see it you can't manage it: In consultation with the operational managers, the information system team developed a web-based reporting system that produced a set of "desert island reports," reports that the operational managers could not imagine living without. Each manager got a set of real-time reports that helped them manage their work and assess their progress. At the start of the work, managers didn't know how many empty homes they had. The new system told them the number of empty homes, the type of property, and when each property was going to be ready for inspection and occupancy. The reports helped operational staff anticipate problems and manage proactively.

The power of positive feedback: As the work progressed, senior managers and elected officials publicly praised and encouraged the staff and tenants involved. Press releases were issued and reports presented to the Council's cabinet meeting. The progress was made visible to residents and other stakeholders through a widely distributed monthly progress report. For many housing services staff, it was the first time they had heard anything good said about their work.

At the start of the improvement program, there were usually about 500 empty properties on any one day. In the first quarter of 2005, there were less than 200. This dramatic reduction has had a number of positive effects:

- 300 extra families have decent, affordable homes;
- 300 sets of neighbors are not living in fear of the crimes that empty properties attract;
- Neighborhoods are less vulnerable to the danger of market collapse that can occur when empty properties begin to accumulate in areas of low demand; and
- There are 300 extra streams of rent income which can be re-invested in housing stock improvements such as energy efficiency.

The success of this work gave staff the confidence to tackle other areas of weakness within the service. It began to restore the confidence of the tenants in the Council's competence as their landlord.

Two years after being judged a failing service, the Housing Inspectorate returned to review progress. Their judgment was that the service was a "fair service with excellent prospects." The report noted the role of strong leadership, a supportive relationship to staff, and a changed organizational culture as contributing to the change. Performance Accountability methods combined with strong leadership turned around a critical service.

Chapter 5:

PUTTING POPULATION AND PERFORMANCE ACCOUNTABILITY TOGETHER

We have now addressed both parts of the Results-Based Accountability framework: Population Accountability and Performance Accountability. In this chapter we will show how they are connected. We will address the contribution that programs make to the quality of life of communities, cities, counties, states and nations. We will look at how community quality of life efforts can, in turn, create connections between programs in the community and provide support for performance improvement efforts.

What is the relationship between programs and community?

Simply stated, customer results contribute to population results. What we do for our customers is our contribution to the quality of life of the community.

Figure 5.1 shows this relationship between Population and Performance Accountability. Population Accountability appears above the horizontal line with results like *Healthy Births* and *Stable Families*. Performance Accountability appears below the horizontal line. Performance measures are shown in the four quadrants for a typical child welfare program.

Notice that above the double line, the rate of child abuse and neglect appears as an indicator. Below the double line, the rate of repeat child abuse and neglect appears as a performance measure. Often, the only difference between a lower right quadrant performance measure and a population indicator is the difference in scale. The same or similar measure addresses customer well-being at the performance level and population well-being at the community level.

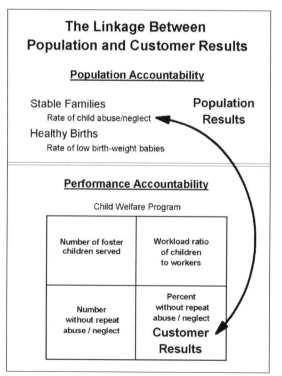

Figure 5.1

This is important for several reasons. First it gives an operational definition to the contribution relationship between customer results and population results. What your program does to prevent repeat child abuse in this case is your contribution to reducing the overall rate of abuse in the community. Second, it allows us to think about the alignment of how we measure program success with how we measure population success. The most important indicators at the community level will often have counterparts in the performance measures of programs. And third, it allows us to avoid the mistake we've been making for 50 years or more of holding programs responsible for producing population level change. Programs can be held responsible for what they do for their customers. Communities must take collective responsibility for the well-being of the children, adults and families who live there.

This relationship between Population and Performance Accountability also shows up in the difference between a program's service population and target population. The service population is made up of the customers who actually receive service from the program. The target population is the group of potential customers from which actual customers are drawn. The target population is always larger than the service population, because it includes many potential customers who are not receiving service. The well-being of target populations is, therefore, part of population and not Performance Accountability. What a program does for its active customers is its contribution to the well-being of the target population of potential customers. Note that the percentage of the target population that is actually receiving service, often referred to as the "percent of need met," is an important *How well did well do it?* measure.

The relationship between programs and populations has been poorly understood in the past. This has lead to repeated demands that programs prove their worth by showing their "impact" at the population level. This is a bogus requirement. Programs can and should show their effects on their customers. They should be able to articulate how their work fits with the work of other partners in a strategy to improve community quality of life. But it is extremely rare that any one program can change population conditions. We must stop asking programs to validate their worth by demonstrating such effects.[94]

Programs and agencies should identify the results and indicators to which they make the most direct contributions. Environmental agencies should track *Clean Environment* and associated indicators. Police departments should track *Safe Communities* and associated indicators. The baselines for these indicators should be on the wall of these agencies. Any presentation made by agency staff and any agency publication should clearly identify these population conditions and the role the agency plays in improving them. After this groundwork is laid, the agency can then address the details of its performance. This will help educate stakeholders about the difference between Population and Performance AccountabilityIt will allow managers to focus on the status

---

[94]. See Demonstrating contribution to community change in Chapter 7 where we discuss how to show the impact of an entire strategy, not just one program, on community results.

of agency performance and what can be done to make it better, without the distraction of unrealistic expectations.

An advanced view of the relationship between indicators and performance measures

Figure 5.2 shows an advanced view of the relationship between population indicators and performance measures. You may have noticed in earlier examples that the measure "high school graduation rate" has been used as both an indicator and a performance measure. It may be somewhat surprising, but some data actually play both roles.

As we go from the program to the agency level, our customer population gets larger. From agency to service system, the customer population gets larger still. As the size of the customer population approaches the total population, the lower right quadrant measures start to have a double life. One minute they are used as performance measures for managing the service system. The next minute they are used as indicators to represent the well-being of a whole population.

The high school graduation rate is a classic example. If a school superintendent convenes a management retreat, the school system's senior staff will go off to a secluded spot to consider the performance of the school system as a service delivery entity. One of the performance measures they will use will be the high school graduation rate. Then the superintendent will leave the management retreat and drive over to the county children's collaborative. Here the collaborative is concerned with the well-being of all children in the county. One of their population results is *All Children Succeed in Life* and one of their indicators is the high school graduation rate. It is the same piece of data playing two different roles.[95]

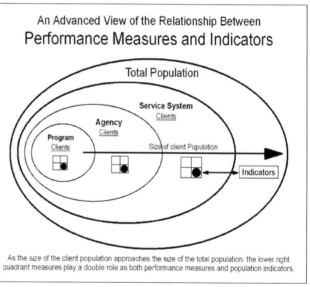

Figure 5.2

This dual role of data is one of the reasons that the distinction between Population and Performance Accountability has been so badly misunderstood. You need to know, when you are using data for management purposes and when you are using data to represent quality of life for a whole population. Sometimes it's the same data.

---

95.   This means that the Montgomery County, Ohio example about school attendance can be considered both a population Turn the Curve story and a performance Turn the Curve story.

One community group created a list of measures and went down the list putting a mark next to each measure to indicate whether it was a performance measure or indicator. Measures are not stamped at birth "indicator" or "performance measure." Measures are categorized based on what questions they answer. When the high school graduation rate answers the question, "Are all our children succeeding in life?" then it is a population indicator. When it answers the question "Is our school system performing well?" then it's a performance measure. Think of it as one actor playing two different roles. This dual role occurs only at the boundary between Performance and Population Accountability. The further from the boundary we go, the more that data tends to play only one role or the other.

The special case of prevention programs

Prevention programs pose an exception to the usual relationship between performance measures and indicators. For most programs, the customer population is a discrete group of people who receive services directly from the program. Prevention programs, by definition, seek to influence the behavior of a large group, most of whom have little or no direct contact with the program. In this case, the target population and the service population are essentially the same.

Take, for example, a county prevention program designed to reduce teen smoking. The program can measure its effect on the customers with whom it has direct contact. When the smoking prevention program makes a presentation at a school assembly, the students in the audience become the customers of the program. The program can measure changes in the attitudes of these students, and where resources permit, actual changes in behavior.

The program would also produce advertising intended to reach all teens. Therefore, all teens in the county could also be considered the program customers. The behavior of teens, such as rate of teen smoking, could be considered a lower right quadrant performance measure.

Many agencies have prevention programs. Health departments seek to prevent disease, in addition to providing treatment. Departments of transportation seek to prevent highway accidents in addition to building and maintaining roads. This is another source of confusion about Population and Performance Accountability. Because the total population can be considered customers for prevention programs, these departments come to believe that the whole population is the customer group for all of its services. The agency sees itself as bearing responsibility for population well-being. This is the set-up for failure we discussed at the beginning of the book where the MASH unit takes responsibility for ending the war.

There is a solution to this problem. Prevention programs, and their host agencies should refrain from adopting population indicators as performance measures. Always track prevention programs using a two part structure that clearly separates Population and Performance Accountability. Treat population results and indicators, like *Healthy Teens* and the percent of teens who smoke, as conditions to which the agency makes a contribution. Then, identify performance measures for the prevention program activities and for customers in direct contact with the program. The next chapter provides formats that can help keep this separation clear. This distinction will also help clarify the important role prevention programs play in organizing and supporting a broader partnership necessary to change population indicators.

Reporting progress on population and performance efforts

Whether you are working on Population or Performance Accountability, it will be necessary to periodically report progress to your stakeholders. There are three types of progress that can be reported. The first type is about numbers and makes use of data for indicators and performance measures.

The second and third types of progress reporting have been around since the beginning of time. They are about accomplishments and stories.

1. Numbers

Population indicators: The rate of teen smoking has been increasing for the past 10 years but has now begun to decline. Turning curves at the population level is a relatively rare event. But it is important to report regularly on the indicator curves we are trying to turn to keep the big picture in focus.

Performance measures: We placed 75% of our trainees in jobs paying better than the minimum wage and 90% of these people still had these jobs six months later. Programs, agencies and service systems should report progress on the most important *How well did we do it?* and *Is anyone better off? measures.*

2. Accomplishments: We opened a new jobs center, hired a new director, implemented a new information system, killed a wooly mammoth, won a national award. Accomplishments are things you have bragging rights to that are not about numbers.

3. Stories or anecdotes illustrate how the lives of individual customers or community members have improved. "Let me tell you about Mrs. Jones...." Combining numbers and stories is the most powerful way to report progress. The stories serve to illustrate what the numbers mean and put a human face on otherwise dry statistics.

All three types of progress should be used in report cards, strategic plans, grant applications and any other form of reporting to stakeholders.

WHERE RESULTS-BASED ACCOUNTABILITY THINKING HAS WORKED

Boston[96]

Boston's work on the juvenile homicide rate has been well documented. The chart at the right shows juvenile homicides in Boston from 1988 to 1998. In the first 5 years, the number of homicides ranged from 6 to 14 per year. It looked like things were getting better with reductions in 1991 and 1992. But in 1993 they set a record of 16 juvenile homicides in one year. People in Boston said, "That's not OK."

What Boston did in response is instructive to any community that wants to turn any curve. They got people around a table. The people at the table included the key city, state and federal law enforcement agencies. It also included juvenile justice, public health, mental health, social services and the schools. The faith community and the business community were represented. Harvard University was at the table.

The group put the baseline for juvenile homicides on the wall. The leaders of the group said in effect,

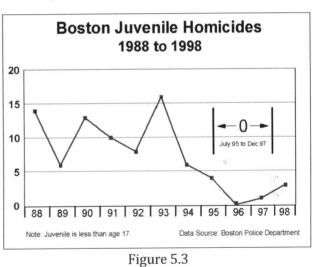

Figure 5.3

We're not here to write press releases about this problem. We're not here to write fancy memorandums of understanding between our agencies. We're here to make these numbers go down. If you have something to contribute to making these numbers go down, you're welcome at this table. If you don't, that's OK. Just find another meeting to go to every month.

---

96. Much of this case example is taken from a lecture given by Lt. France from the Boston City Police Department at a national conference in San Diego in 1999. Many reports and articles have been published on the Boston story, including: Braga, Anthony A., David M. Kennedy, Anne M. Piehl, and Elin J. Waring, National Institute of Justice Research Report Reducing Gun Violence: The Boston Gun Project's Operation Ceasefire, September 2001. See also ksg.harvard.edu/criminaljustice/research/bgp.htm for additional citations.

They worked for 12 to 15 months to develop and implement a strategy to make the numbers go down. Part of that strategy was an attack on the most violent gang in Boston. They did the undercover and other work necessary to take down the Intervale gang. They prosecuted the "shooters" in that gang under federal racketeering (RICO) statutes. Before that, prosecutions under state law had lead to short stays in the state prison where gang members would visit their friends and quickly get back on the street. Federal prosecution meant they would serve 90% of their sentence in a jail in Texas. That was different.

There were also many positive parts to their plan. They had a recreation component. This is where you first might have heard about "midnight basketball." They had a jobs program, a mentoring program, and a tutoring program. Perhaps most importantly, they demonstrated to the gang community that they were all working together and gang members could no longer play one agency off against another.

Together the partners produced an effect that none of them would have believed if you'd told them at the beginning: zero juvenile homicides from July 1995 to December 1997. Two and one half years, zero! I don't care what forecasting technique you use, zero was not in the cards. It could be argued that there were twenty young people alive, who would not have been, had Boston not done this work.

Boston came together and turned a curve. Like Tillamook County, Boston has had a rebound in these numbers. There has been a debate about whether Boston's approach is better or worse than New York City's Compstat system for tracking and driving down crime rates. The important point is what Boston's experience has **in common** with New York's Compstat and with Baltimore's Citystat and similar efforts across the country. They all use data as a catalyst at the beginning of the process. They work to understand the story behind the baselines. They draw together a diverse group of partners. They consider what works. And they take action. These are the essential elements of RBA.

Chapter 6:

MANAGEMENT, BUDGETING AND STRATEGIC PLANNING AS A SINGLE SYSTEM

In this chapter we address a second mental model that concerns the ways in which we organize management, budgeting and strategic planning processes. These three processes are found in all organizations to one degree or another:

Management: the day-to-day and month-to-month running of the operation;
Budgeting: the annual (or multi-year) decision making process about resources;
Strategic planning: the two to ten year[97] decision making process about direction.

We have come to think of management, budgeting and strategic planning as separate processes. They often reside in different parts of the organization. Budgeting is in the budget shop. Strategic planning is in the planning division. Management is in the executive office and the job duties of managers and supervisors. With RBA we can begin to think about management, budgeting and strategic planning as three parts of a single system.

Figure 6.1 (taken from work with the state of Wyoming and the city of Louisville) shows how RBA can help align and unify these three components.

Management: Managers can use the Performance Accountability 7 Questions on a monthly or quarterly basis to assess performance and create action plans to improve performance.

Budgeting: The budget director can use the 7 Questions in the annual budget process to organize internal budget hearings and display proposed and final budgets (See the budget format from San Mateo County in Figure 6.3).

Strategic Planning: Strategic planning is displayed in two parts in the schematic. Population level strategic planning looks at improving the quality of life in an entire city, county, state or nation and sets out strategies that include, but are not limited to government. Department level strategic planning addresses the performance of the governmental and non-governmental agencies within those geographic areas. Organizations can answer the 7 Questions for a two to ten year period and make decisions about long term direction.

---

97. Contrast typical 2 to 10 year strategic planning with the Native American concept of responsibility for 7 generations: your grandchildren's grandchildren's grandchildren - a powerful idea that could be represented with a version of the symbol: |-|-|-|.

Surprisingly, the most important of these three processes is **management**. If you use data on a day to day basis to run your organization, then once a year you spin out the budget. Once every two or three years you create a strategic plan. The use of data in budgets and strategic plans becomes a **by-product** of good management practice.

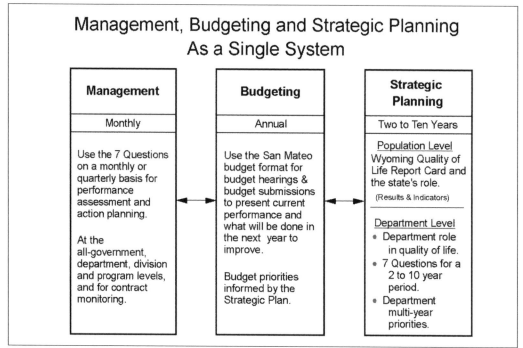

Figure 6.1

Results-based management

We have already addressed the essential elements of results-based management in Chapter 4. The heart of good management is good supervision. Good supervision involves setting expectations and holding subordinates accountable for meeting those expectations.[98] The Performance Accountability 7 Questions can be used for these purposes.

Results-based budgeting[99]

Let's use government budgeting as a lens through which to assess current budgeting practice across the public and private sectors. At least three significant weaknesses are commonly found in current government budget processes.

---

[98]   See "A complete course in supervision in 5 minutes" on resultsaccountability.com.
[99]   See the following publications for more detail on Results Based Budgeting: "From Outcomes to Budgets: An Approach to Outcome (or Result) Based Budgeting for Family and Children's Services," Mark Friedman, Center for the Study of Social Policy, July, 1995; "A Strategy Map for Results-based Budgeting: Moving from Theory to Practice," The Finance Project, Mark Friedman, September, 1996; and "A Guide to Developing and Using Family and Children's Budgets," The Finance Project, Mark Friedman and Anna Danegger, August, 1998.

Shortsighted: Most government budgets are short term, one or two year plans, with little systematic consideration of long term trends. We know that investments in prevention sometimes take years to show up. Providing effective health care in early childhood, for example, pays off in healthier adolescents, greater success in school and more productive and self sufficient adulthood. Shortsighted budgets often block us from making important investments just because they don't pay off in one or two years.

Fragmented: Current budgets are badly fragmented. It is necessary to have spending plans by agency and program since agencies must be held accountable for the public funds in their custody. However, budgets that are organized solely by agency and program make it hard to consider matters that cross over agency or program lines, such as the well-being of children or the performance of service systems. Government organization is often a maze of interrelated, overlapping and sometimes duplicative structures. These structures tend to carve up and compartmentalize people and systems, rather than dealing with whole people and whole systems. Legislative branch committee structures usually mirror executive branch organization, and compound the problem.

Process, not results oriented: Finally, budgeting systems tend to be slavishly devoted to process and not results. This is partly a function of the sheer magnitude of the task of developing spending plans for a large enterprise every year or two. This effort often leaves little time for work beyond the minimum. Even the best budget shops are hard pressed to meet the procedural demands of the annual document production line. The laws governing budget processes usually do not require long term consideration of the well-being of children, elders or any other population.

These are some of the reasons why our elected leaders become so frustrated with government in general and government budgeting in particular. The problems they were elected to solve are so fragmented and buried in process that it is often difficult to connect budget decisions to the improved well-being of their constituents and communities.

A fully developed results-based budgeting process would build on, not supplant, existing budget structures. It would connect the decision making processes to both customer and population results. It would provide system-wide and community-wide pictures of spending. It would also provide an audit trail between spending plans and the quality of life conditions they are intended to improve.

Results based budgeting does not guarantee that results will improve. Budgeting is about making choices. Using results-based budgeting means that you will **have** better choices. It doesn't necessarily mean that you will **make** better choices. The problems of child abuse, teen pregnancy, school failure and economic dependency cannot be easily solved, and results-based budgeting is no panacea. In the end, we might not have the know-how, the resources or the will to solve these problems. But budget systems geared to changing results are **more likely** to succeed than the scatter shot approach embodied in our current systems.

Budgets of the future will have two parts (See Figure 6.2). Volume I will be organized by population results. There will be one page for each result (e.g. *Clean Environment, Safe Communities, Children Ready for School*). This page will show the baselines for the most important indicators, the story behind these baselines and our overall strategy for getting better.

Volume II will be organized as it is now, by department, division, and program. The budget for each level of the department will have the same structure. The budget will show the three most important performance measures, the story behind performance and the strategy to improve performance.

The challenge at all levels is not to let the number of performance measures explode. At the department, division and program levels, only the three to five most important measures should be presented. If more performance measures are needed, they can be presented in a separate appendix.

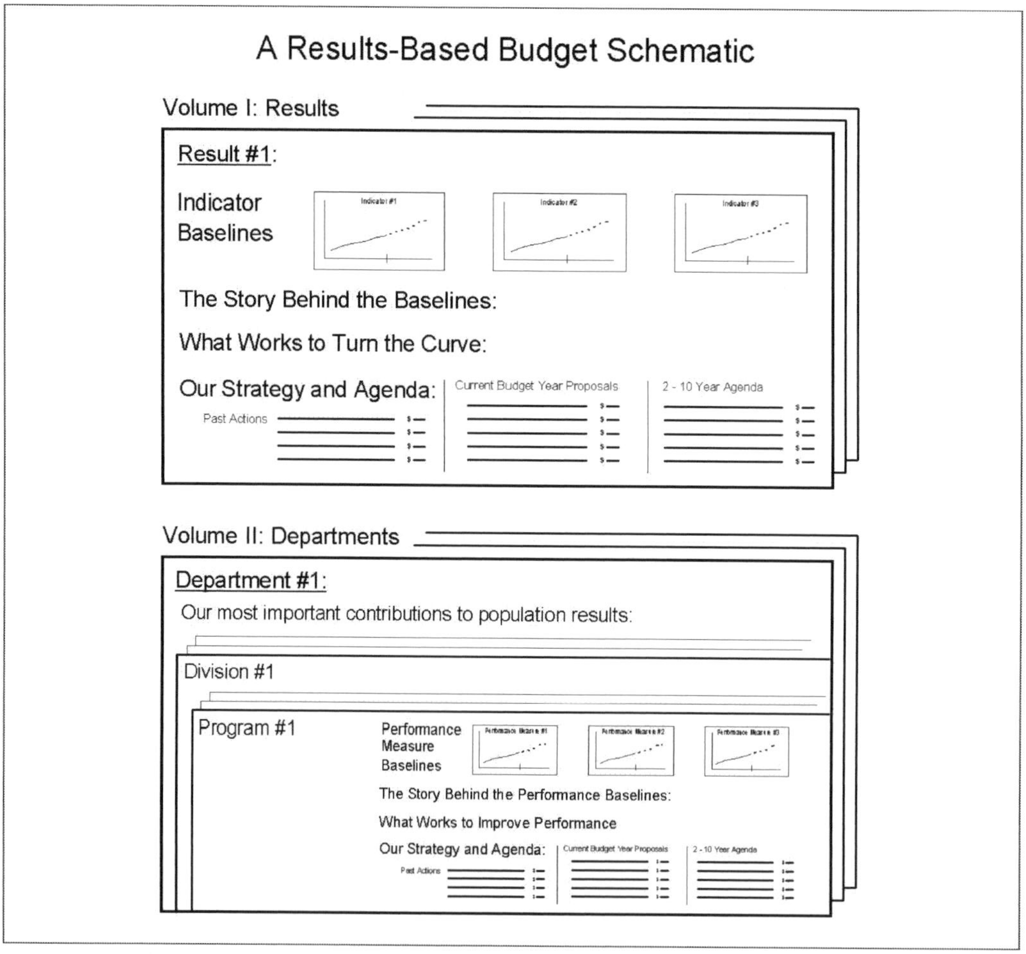

Figure 6.2

Look at the budgets that are touted as national models. When you get to the department level, there are dozens if not hundreds of measures. It is impossible to hold an agency manager accountable if you do not know which measures are most important. RBA methods can be used to identify the three to five measures that constitute an agency's bottom line. The legislative branch budget hearing process should focus on how the agency and its programs contribute to quality of life, what the agency proposes to do to improve performance on its headline performance measures, and how these plans are reflected in the budget.

If you are a fan of chaos and complexity theory, you will notice that this budget structure is a fractal.[100] It's the same pattern of thinking and presentation at every level from the big picture view of population well-being to the smallest part of the bureaucracy and everything in between. One of the powers of this way of thinking about accountability is that you don't have to teach people different ways to do the work depending on where they are in the system. It's the same leaking roof thinking process at every level.

San Mateo County, California has pioneered the use of RBA methods in budgeting.[101] Here's an excerpt from their 2005-2006 Budget. The first page shows a program mission or purpose statement. San Mateo County uses the word "outcome" to label this idea. Then they show the historical part of the baselines for two performance measures and two years of targets. The next section provides a place to describe services and present accomplishments. Next the story behind the baseline performance is presented. And finally, the program presents its priorities for the coming fiscal years. It's a simple, common sense format that is easily understood by decision makers and the lay public. The next page of the budget (not shown here) presents additional performance measures for the program. These measures are organized into the three RBA categories: *How much did we do? How well did we do it? Is anyone better off?* These are the official government categories for performance measures in San Mateo County and a growing number of other jurisdictions.

San Mateo County also has the equivalent of a Volume I report where community-wide results and county efforts to improve quality of life are presented periodically. Taken together, these are among the best formats for presenting budgets in the country. This achievement was recognized by the Government Finance Officers Association with their 2004 award for budget presentation.

[100.] For those interested in more about the parallel to fractal geometry, see Chaos, Making a New Science, James Gleick, 1987. See also the Epilogue "On the Edge" for a discussion of the relationship between RBA and Chaos and Complexity theory.

[101.] To view the entire San Mateo County budget presentation go to: co.sanmateo.ca.us/smc/department/ home/0,,1909_222285,00.html

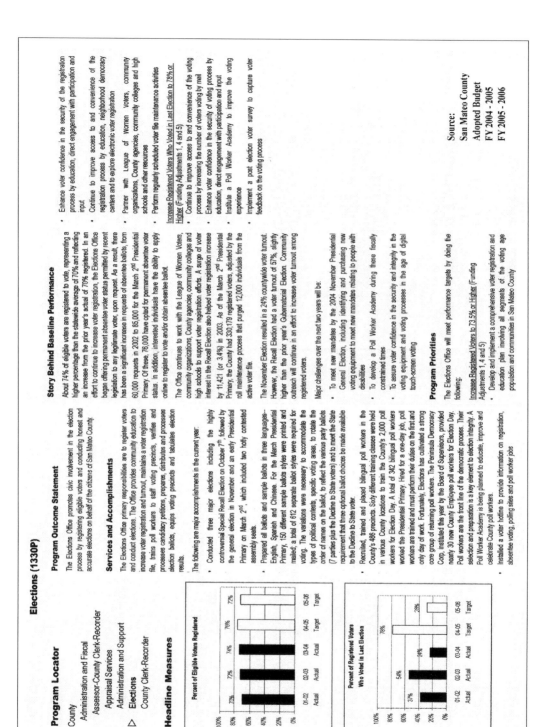

Elections (1330P)

Program Locator

County
Administration and Fiscal
Assessor-County Clerk-Recorder
Appraisal Services
Administration and Support
△ Elections
County Clerk-Recorder

Headline Measures

Percent of Eligible Voters Registered

01-02 Actual	02-03 Actual	03-04 Actual	04-05 Target	05-06 Target
70%	72%	74%	79%	72%

Percent of Registered Voters Who Voted in Last Election

01-02 Actual	02-03 Actual	03-04 Actual	04-05 Target	05-06 Target
37%	54%	24%	79%	20%

Program Outcome Statement

The Elections Office promotes civic involvement in the election process by registering eligible voters and conducting honest and accurate elections on behalf of the citizens of San Mateo County.

Services and Accomplishments

The Elections Office primary responsibilities are to register voters and conduct elections. The Office provides community education to increase voter registration and turnout, maintains a voter registration file, trains poll workers to staff voting precincts, verifies and processes candidacy petitions, prepares, distributes and processes election ballots, equips voting precincts and tabulates election results.

The following are major accomplishments in the current year:

- Conducted three major elections including the highly controversial Special Recall Election on October 7th, followed by the general election in November and an early Presidential Primary on March 2nd, which included two hotly contested assembly seats.

- Prepared all ballots and sample ballots in three languages—English, Spanish and Chinese. For the March Presidential Primary, 150 different sample ballots styles were printed and mailed; a total of 612 separate ballot styles were required for voting. The variations were necessary to accommodate the types of political contests, specific voting areas, to rotate the order of names on the ballot, to reflect the various party ballots (7 parties plus the Decline to State voters) and to meet the State requirement that three optional ballot choices be made available to the Decline to State voter.

- Recruited, trained and placed bilingual poll workers in the County's 486 precincts. Sixty different training classes were held in various County locations to train the County's 2,000 poll workers for Election Day. A total of 342 bilingual poll workers worked the Presidential Primary. Hired for a one-day job, poll workers are trained and must perform their duties on the first and only day of work. Fortunately, Elections has cultivated a strong core group of returning poll workers. The Peninsula Democracy Corp, instituted this year by the Board of Supervisors, provided nearly 30 new County Employee poll workers for Election Day. Poll workers are the front line of the democratic process. Their selection and preparation is a key element to election integrity. A Poll Worker Academy is being planned to educate, improve and celebrate County poll workers.

- Installed a voter hotline to provide information on registration, absentee voting, polling sites and poll worker jobs.

Story Behind Baseline Performance

About 74% of eligible voters are registered to vote, representing a higher percentage than the statewide average of 70% and reflecting an increase from the prior year's actual of 70% registered. In an effort to continue to increase voter registration, the Elections Office began offering permanent absentee voter status permitted by recent legislation to any legitimate voter, upon request. As a result, there has been a significant increase in requests of absentee ballots, from 60,000 requests in 2002 to 85,000 for the March 2nd Presidential Primary. Of these, 76,000 have opted for permanent absentee voter status. In addition, interested individuals have the ability to apply online to register to vote and/or obtain absentee ballot.

The Office continues to work with the League of Women Voters, community organizations, County agencies, community colleges and high schools to support voter registration efforts. A surge of voter interest in the Recall Election also helped voter registration increase by 11,421 (or 3.4%) in 2003. As of the March 2nd Presidential Primary, the County had 330,179 registered voters, adjusted by the roll maintenance process that purged 12,000 individuals from the active voter file.

The November Election resulted in a 24% countywide voter turnout. However, the Recall Election had a voter turnout of 57%, slightly higher than the prior year's Gubernatorial Election. Community outreach will continue in an effort to increase voter turnout among registered voters.

Major challenges over the next two years will be:

- To meet new mandates by the 2004 November Presidential General Election, including identifying and purchasing new voting equipment to meet new mandates relating to people with disabilities
- To develop a Poll Worker Academy during these fiscally constrained times
- To assure voter confidence in the security and integrity in the voting equipment and voting processes in the age of digital touch-screen voting

Program Priorities

The Elections Office will meet performance targets by doing the following:

Increase Registered Voters to 73.5% or Higher (Funding Adjustments 1, 4 and 5)

- Develop and implement a comprehensive voter registration and education plan involving all segments of the voting age population and communities in San Mateo County
- Enhance voter confidence in the security of the registration process by education, direct engagement with participation and input
- Continue to improve access to and convenience of the registration process by education, neighborhood democracy centers and to explore electronic voter registration
- Partner with League of Women Voters, community organizations, County agencies, community colleges and high schools and other resources
- Perform regularly scheduled voter file maintenance activities

Increase Registered Voters Who Voted in Last Election to 78% or Higher (Funding Adjustments 1, 4 and 5)

- Continue to improve access to and convenience of the voting process by increasing the number of voters voting by mail
- Enhance voter confidence in the security of voting process by education, direct engagement with participation and input
- Institute a Poll Worker Academy to improve the voting experience
- Implement a post election voter survey to capture voter feedback on the voting process

Source:
San Mateo County
Adopted Budget
FY 2004 - 2005
FY 2005 - 2006

Figure 6.3

Children's budgets

There are two components of results-based budgeting that are specific to the well-being of children and families: a Children's Budget and a Cost of Bad Results analysis. Let's look at the children's budget first. The concepts used to create a children's budget can be applied to budgets for other special populations, including elders, veterans, ethnic groups and people with disabilities.

A children's budget is a document that summarizes spending for children and their families for a community, city, county, state or nation. It is a decision-making tool that can help make sense of how resources are currently being used and make the case for investments in child and family wellbeing.

Making sense of spending for children and families is not an easy task. Spending for children and families is spread across different levels of government (federal, state, county, city, school district), across many agencies within each level, and across the public and private sectors. It involves dozens of funding sources that pay for hundreds of different programs. This fragmented system of funding reflects a more profound fragmentation of services, based on categories of children and categories of service. While this system does a good job of helping some children, it also fails many children.

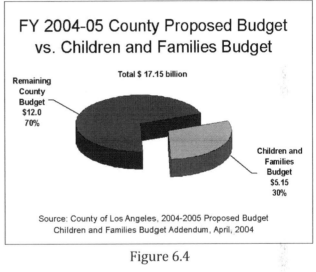

FY 2004-05 County Proposed Budget vs. Children and Families Budget

Total $ 17.15 billion

Remaining County Budget $12.0 70%

Children and Families Budget $5.15 30%

Source: County of Los Angeles, 2004-2005 Proposed Budget Children and Families Budget Addendum, April, 2004

Figure 6.4

A children's budget can help unravel this complex puzzle. See the excerpt from the Los Angeles County Children and Families Budget in Figure 6.4.[102] A children's budget can answer seemingly simple questions like: How much are we spending on children and family services? Are costs increasing or decreasing? Are spending priorities changing over time? It can also answer more complex questions like: Are children receiving their fair share of funding? Are we investing enough in the future well-being of children? Are they protected more or less than other parts of the budget in times of cutbacks? How does our spending for children's services compare to other jurisdictions?

[102.] Thanks to David E. Janssen, Chief Administrative Officer, Los Angeles County and Deena Margolis, lead budget officer responsible for creating the Los Angeles County Children and Families Budget.

In total, we are spending a lot of money on children and families. A large percent of that spending is for remediating problems after they occur. This means that we are paying more for remediation than we would if we invested in child and family well-being before problems occur. There is a growing consensus that substantive investments in early childhood development and family support services are not only good social policy but good fiscal policy as well. Children's budgets can help us understand our choices and act on our investment opportunities.

A simple version of a children's budget can be produced in one year, but the full development typically takes two to three years. In the first year, budgets should display an inventory of spending for children and families by agency and program. This provides an overview of how spending is distributed across the organizational landscape and how spending patterns are changing by agency. In more advanced versions, spending is disaggregated by common service categories, such as child care, and by function such as intake and assessment or out-of-home care. These more advanced budgets allow consideration of the adequacy of various services and ways to make the configuration of the service system more efficient. The most advanced version of a children's budget goes on to include a report on results and indicators and investment choices for improving child and family well-being.

It is very important to consider the ways that the children's budget will be used before starting the process of constructing one. Will it be used for policy analysis, advocacy or decision-making? What are the most important questions to be answered? What data do you need to answer these questions? Without this advanced planning there is a risk that the document won't get used.

A surprisingly large number of states and localities have created different forms of children's budgets in the last 20 years. At least 30 states, counties and cities have, at one time or another, produced such a document.[103] Among the best examples are children's budgets from Contra Costa County, Los Angeles County, Philadelphia, San Francisco, Maryland, Oklahoma and Kansas. These provide exemplary formats and have a history of being used in advocacy and decision-making processes. A full description of how to produce such a document is provided in the Finance Project paper "A Guide to Developing and Using Family and Children's Budgets."

Cost of bad results

Ben Franklin's famous saying, "An ounce of prevention is worth a pound of cure,"[104] is an old part of our culture. But Ben might agree that it would help to know the cost of what we were preventing. How much cure do we get for our one ounce of investment?

[103.] See Appendix A from "A Guide to Developing and Using Family and Children's Budgets," Friedman and Danneger, The Finance Project, August, 1998.

[104.] This footnote intentionally left blank.

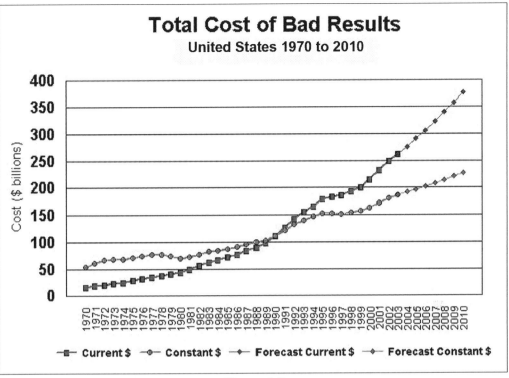

Figure 6.5

Ben suggested a 16 to 1 return on investment, and people have found that a credible ratio for the last 200 years.[105]

The cost of bad results is the cost of child and family problems we are trying to prevent. Most of the money that government spends on children and families, other than elementary and secondary education, is for **bad** results. This spending is for children who are **not** ready for school, **not** succeeding in school, **not** staying out of trouble, and for families that are **not** stable and **not** self sufficient. The cost of bad results shows up in everything from government expenditures for child abuse services to the portion of our monthly insurance bills caused by crime related damage.

Figure 6.5 shows my estimate of the total United States cost of bad results from 1970 to 2003, and the forecasted total for 2004 to 2010. The total cost of bad results was approximately $260 billion in 2003. At this annual rate of growth, the total is likely to have exceeded $350 billion per year at the end of the decade.[106]

---

[105] The 3 to 1 return typically found in longitudinal studies of investments in child development, such as the Perry Preschool study, seems modest by comparison.

[106] It is possible to quickly derive a comparable estimate for any given jurisdiction by taking a population share of the national totals.

These estimates were derived by adding all federal state and local expenditures for welfare, juvenile justice and child welfare, plus the child and family share of Medicaid health care (approximately one third), one half of all adult law enforcement and corrections costs,[107] and one half of all private charitable expenditures for human services.[108] This is a **conservative estimate** that leaves out significant other costs like the mental health costs not included in Medicaid, the cost of public housing programs, homeless services, energy assistance, workforce development, and prenatal nutrition programs. It also excludes other costs that are harder to quantify like the education costs caused by poor birth outcomes, and the societal costs of alcoholism[109] and drug abuse.[110]

The following question was used to guide the choices about what to include and not include: **"What service expenditures do we want to reduce because there is less need for the service?"** When the question is posed this way, entire programs can be counted. Total welfare, foster care, and juvenile justice expenditures are included. We want welfare, foster care and juvenile justice expenditures to decrease because there are fewer families who need government help, fewer children who cannot live safely with their families and less juvenile crime. The "less need" language is important because some expenditures, such as those for child abuse and domestic violence, may increase in the short run because we find cases that now go unreported.

By asking a second question, it is possible to identify the size of our current investment in prevention. **"What expenditures are currently devoted to reducing the cost of bad results?"** This somewhat more complicated way of framing the questions avoids problems that go with trying to directly identify prevention spending. If you announce that you are creating an analysis that separates prevention and non-prevention spending, everyone quickly realizes that it's much better to be counted as a prevention program. Everything becomes a prevention program. The prisons are prevention programs because they prevent recidivism. The analysis quickly becomes meaningless.

With the questions as written, no one can argue that total prisons costs are part of the cost of bad results. We want prison expenditures to go down because there are fewer people who need to be incarcerated. The second question helps identify those program components designed to reduce the cost of bad results. Vocational training pro-

---

[107] I have not been able to locate any research on the percent of those in the adult corrections system who had some involvement with the juvenile justice system. From talking with corrections officials, 50% seems a conservative estimate.

[108] Sources: Statistical Abstract of the United States 1994, 1997, 2004-5, House Ways and Means Committee Green Book 2004, Medicaid Source Book 2004.

[109] In a 1997 report, the State of Maine estimated the annual cost of alcoholism to be $1 billion per year in Maine alone. See http://pressherald.mainetoday.com/specialrpts/alcohol/d8summ.htm

[110] Anyone willing to create a more complete analysis, considering these other factors, would make an important contribution.

grams within prisons are counted here. We also count family preservation services designed to keep families safely together and Medicaid funded preventive health care designed to reduce long term treatment costs.

It may seem that this construction of the cost of bad results plays into the hands of those who advocate cutting back on social spending. Using the formula offered here, less social spending produces a lower total cost of bad results. To reduce the cost of bad results, just cut social spending. But, reduced social spending is not always bad. In fact, what we really hope for is a reduction in spending that reflects **less need** for services. No one argues that the reduced cost of welfare is a good thing when it follows from a recession ending and people going back to work. If we are successful in preventing child abuse, domestic violence, and teen pregnancy, then we will be able to reduce expenditures for the services that address these problems, freeing up resources to be used for other improvements in the quality of life of children, families and communities.

Hacking away at the social safety net would drive these costs down in the short run, but would almost certainly cost more in the long run. One of the periods of greatest dis-investment in the social safety net occurred with the US federal budgets cuts in 1981. Consider the cohort of all children aged 0 to 5 in 1981. During the four year period (1990 to 1993) when these children were 9 to 17 years old, the Cost of Bad Results grew at the fastest rate of any four year period in the last 30 years.[111] This may be coincidence. But we know that late childhood and adolescence are the most expensive years in terms of bad results. Could this extraordinary growth in costs be the delayed effect of disinvestment in children and families from the early 1980's? What happened to the class of 1981? A more complete analysis might confirm that the cuts in spending in 1981 contributed to these higher costs a decade later.

The cost of bad results appears to be growing faster than revenue. Between 1990 and 2003, state and local government receipts grew by 76%, and federal government receipts grew by 73%[112] compared to an increase in the cost of bad results of 134%. What happens when the cost of remediating problems grows faster than revenue? Something has to give. That something is prevention. We don't have to pay for prevention today. We can pay for prevention tomorrow. Today we have to build the prison. Today we have to pay the foster care and Medicaid bills. So we systematically underfund or even de-fund prevention investments. This means that the remediation costs grow faster. The convergence of costs and resources happens faster. One day, public budgets may be made up of nothing but remedial costs.

---

[111]   The four year rate was 36.5%, or 8.1% per year. This four year period spans beyond the recession of 1990-91. The 8.1 % growth rate was significantly higher than the average annual growth of 3.5 % between 1970 and 1989, and 5.3% growth between 1993 and 2003, including three other periods of recession: 1973-75, 1980-82 and 2001-02.

[112]   *Statistical Abstract of the United States 2004-2005*, Tables 420 and 461.

Wyoming Strategic Planning Design - Part I

(To be completed by the Governors Planning Deptartment)

Quality of Life Result:

Examples: A Clean Environment, A Prosperous Economy, Strong Stable Families, Children Ready for and Succeeding in School, etc.

Why is this important?

Briefly explain, so a taxpayer could understand, why this quality of life condition is important to the people of Wyoming.

How are we doing?

Show the 3 to 5 most important indicators in the form of baselines with at least 3 years of actual history. Optional: provide a 2 year forecast at current effort level.

The story behind the baselines:

Explain, so a taxpayer could understand, the causes behind the indicator baselines above. Use additional data as necessary to tell this story.

What it will take to do better and the role of state government:

Include no-cost and low-cost ideas and the role of the state's partners.

Appendix A: Data development Agenda: List priorities for new or better indicator data.

Figure 6.6

Wyoming Strategic Planning Design - Part II
Same format for Departments, Divisions and Programs

Department/Division/Program:

Contribution to Wyoming Quality of Life:

Briefly explain, so a taxpayer could understand, how your (Dept/Div/Prog), in conjunction with other public and private partners, contributes to the quality of life of the people of Wyoming.

Basic Facts:

Show total number of staff and size of budget in total and general funds.
List the 5 most important programs or functions and show annual number served.

Performance:

Show the 3 to 5 most important performance measures in the form of baselines with at least 3 years of actual history. Optional: provide a 2 year forecast of performance at current effort level. Performance measures must be those that best answer the questions:
- How well are we delivering service?
- Are our customers better off? (Customer Results)

Story behind (last 3 years of) performance:

Briefly explain, so a taxpayer could understand, the causes behind your performance for the last few years, including an explanation of the picture of performance shown in the baselines above. Reference your accomplishments where they have contributed to improved performance. Use additional performance data as necessary to tell this story. Best formatting is short paragraphs with first sentence underlined.

What do you propose to do to improve performance in the next 2 yrs?

Include no-cost and low-cost ideas and the contribution of partners. Best formatting is short paragraphs with action item underlined.

Appendix A: Data development Agenda: List priorities for new or better data on performance.

Appendix B: Link to Budget: Provide detail on priorities identified above which are included in the current or proposed budget.

Figure 6.7

Given current social and fiscal policies, we will have spent **$250 billion**[113] **above current spending levels** between 2006 and 2010 on the cost of bad results. What investments could we make today that would turn the curve on these kinds of future costs? Federal, state and local budgets should include annual cost of bad results analyses and recommendations on how to reduce these costs.

Results-based strategic planning

In many organizations, strategic planning processes are completely useless. Strategic plans often take a lot of time and energy to produce and simply don't get used for anything. RBA offers a way to produce useful plans.

Strategic plans should have two parts, a population part and a performance part. The state of Wyoming has used this two-part approach.[114] The Wyoming strategic planning design is shown in Figures 6.6 and 6.7. Part I of the strategic plan shows how the state as a whole is doing on the most important population results. For each result (e.g. Clean Environment, Prosperous Economy, Stable Families) the structure provides a place to describe what is meant by the result and why it is important to the people of Wyoming. The next section, "How are we doing?" provides space for the three to five most important indicator baselines along with the story behind those baselines.

The last question is, "What will it take to do better and what is the role of state government?" This is a powerful construction of the "What Works?" question. What will it take to improve environmental quality? What will it take to get all children ready for school? And what is the role of government in these larger strategies? The question makes clear that government by itself cannot produce a clean environment or make all children ready for school. This question about the government's contribution provides an opportunity to think about a larger strategy involving many partners without assuming full responsibility.

Part II shows how each department, division or program is performing. The section at the top of part II (Contribution to Quality of Life) provides a link between performance and population quality of life.

The section on basic facts provides space for the raw counts of customers, staff and dollars. The basic facts will usually come from *How much did we do?* measures.

The performance section shows the baselines for the three to five most important *How well did we do it?* and *Is anyone better off?* measures. The story behind performance explains the causes of past and current performance, in terms that taxpayers and voters can understand. The last section provides space to describe what will be done to improve performance in the next two years.

---

113. In current dollars.
114. Thanks to the Wyoming Governor's office.

This strategic planning structure exactly parallels the structure of the budget presentation in the previous section which in turn parallels the structure of day to day and month to month management processes in the 7 Questions. This makes it possible to completely align management, budgeting and strategic planning. More importantly, it allows these separate processes to be mutually reinforcing and useful.

Unified planning for education

No field suffers so much from overlapping and duplicative planning requirements as public education. Schools and school districts all across the country are required to complete many different plans, often putting essentially the same content in different formats.

RBA provides a method to align education planning requirements and avoid duplicating effort. An Approach to Unified Planning for Education is shown in Figure 6.8. It starts with seven student and school goals[115] commonly found in local education plans.

- All students are proficient in reading, math, and science.
- All teachers are highly qualified.
- All English Language Learners (ELL) are proficient in reading, math, and science.
- All students are safe and drug free.
- All students graduate from high school.
- All parents are involved.
- Technology supports student achievement.

Under the unified planning approach, the school or school district would form a planning group for each goal. The groups would identify three to five performance measures for each goal, gather data and create baselines for each measure. The groups would then consider the story behind the baselines, identify partners with a role to play, explore what works to turn the curves and develop an action plan for each goal. Some elements of the action plan will be specific to one goal and some will be cross-cutting actions that will contribute to improvement on several goals. In plan presentations, cross-cutting actions can be specially organized, coded or colored to show their greater importance. A separate set of appendices for demographics, secondary measures and other supporting documentation can be developed to carry much of the detail that now clutters up plans and detracts from their clarity and utility.

These seven strands of work, taken together, represent a comprehensive plan for school improvement. The strands can be reassembled in different combinations to produce any of the plans the school is required to submit. The top of Figure 6.8 shows the eight plans commonly required of schools and school districts in Arizona. The "x"

---

[115]   The word "goal" is commonly used in the education community to describe student or school results, and we will use that word throughout the rest of this section.

UNIFIED PLANNING FOR EDUCATION

Required Plans	All students are proficient in reading, math and science.	All teachers are highly qualified.	All ELL students are proficient in reading, math and science.	All students are safe and drug free.	All students graduate from high school.	All parents are involved.	Technology supports student achievement.
Consolidated Plan	X				X	X	
School Improvement Plan	X	X	X	X	X	X	
Technology Plan						X	X
Professional Development		X					
301 Plan		X					
NCA Accreditation	X	X					X
District Assessment Plan	X	X					
School Reform Plan	X						
Customer Results or Goals	All students are proficient in reading, math and science.	All teachers are highly qualified.	All ELL students are proficient in reading, math and science.	All students are safe and drug free.	All students graduate from high school.	All parents are involved.	Technology supports student achievement.
Performance Measures	Percent proficient	Percent highly qualified	Percent proficient	Rate of drug use	Graduation rate	Percent involved	Percent students & teachers technology literate
Baselines							
Story							
Partners							
What Works	→	→	→	→	→	→	→
Action Plan	→	→	→	→	→	→	→

Prepared for the Arizona Department of Education by the Fiscal Policy Studies Institute, March, 2004.

Figure 6.8

marks show which strands go with which plans. Under this process, the planning is done once, using the same RBA process for each strand. This makes the plans easier to produce and easier to understand and use.

This approach to unified planning is still only a theory. Someday a state department of education or some rebellious school district will adopt this approach and relieve some of the burden now imposed by duplicative education planning processes. The time freed up by simplified planning can go back into helping children succeed in school.

Results-based grantmaking[116]

It is hard to speak the truth about grantmaking. As one foundation executive put it: "Since I joined the foundation world, I haven't had a bad idea or a bad lunch."

Most funders[117] preach account-ability, but not many practice it well. Most funders fail to distin-guish between Population and Performance Accountability, and create unrealistic expecta-tions about what their grants and grantees can accomplish. Many funders impose complex reporting requirements on their grantees but often don't use simple accountability practices in running their own organiza-tions. RBA methods can make the work of grantmaking more clear, realistic and effective.

Organizations Still Waiting
for their first foundation grant

1. Institute for the Study of Spontaneity (ISS)
2. Center for the Study of Study Centers (CSSC)
3. National Association of Foundation Grantees (NAFOG)
4. Center for Wishful Thinking (CWIT)
5. Technical Assistance Center for Congressional Amity (TACCY)
6. Federation of Organizations with Good Intentions (FOGI)
7. Overhead is Us (IOU) (Also known as Us is Over Our Head)
8. Center for Misleading Data (COMAND)
9. Ctr. for Sht. Trm. Thnkng (CISTT)
10. Hindsight Inc. (HINDINC)

FPSI

Figure 6.9

First, funders need to sort out what population results they are seeking to affect in the communities, cities, counties or states in which they make grants. Funders and their grantees can then have an honest conversation about what it means to produce pop-ulation level change and avoid over-promising what can be accomplished.

---

116. For more on this subject, see "Results Based Grantmaking, An Approach to Decision Mak-ing for Foundations and Other Funders," FPSI, October, 2000.

117. For purposes of this discussion, funders include charitable foundations, United Ways, and government agencies that award grants.

Performance Accountability methods can be used to track the performance of both the grantees and the funder's organization. How well are the grantee agencies performing? Are the grantees on time and on budget with their funded activities? Are the grantees making a difference in the lives of the people directly served with grant dollars? For the funder's organization: Are contracts and invoices processed on time? What percent of authorized grant funds are expended? Are grantees satisfied with the support they receive from the funder? And most importantly, what percent of grants have a turn the curve story to tell?

Figure 6.10 provides an overview of Results Based Grantmaking. Funders should decide on a set of results and indicators that they seek to affect such as *A Safe community,* or *A Clean Environment.* The funder should identify a complete strategy to turn the curves and then decide on their role inside this strategy.

Funders consistently skip the step of identifying a complete strategy and go directly from population results to their grantmaking agenda. They create the impression, and sometimes even believe that their grantmaking agenda by itself can change population results. It almost never can. Funders, like foundations and United Ways are uniquely situated to

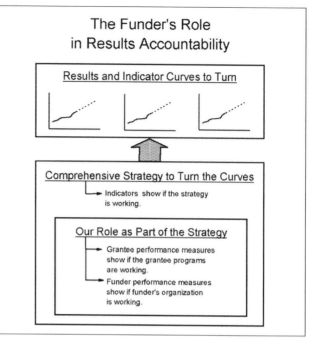

Figure 6.10

Results-Based Grantmaking
for Foundations and Other Funders

1. What quality of life conditions (results) do we seek to improve in the communities (cities, counties, states, nations) where we make grants?

2. What would these conditions look like if we could see them?

3. How can we measure these conditions?

4. How are the communities doing on the most important of these measures?

5. Who are the partners that have a role to play in doing better?

6. What would it take to do better? What strategy should the community as a whole pursue?

7. What is our role inside that strategy?

Figure 6.11

think about complete strategies. They are sometimes the only ones with the time or the neutral perspective to think about "what would it take?"

I first came to understand this problem when I was working with a foundation that was trying to reduce rates of violence in a large metropolitan county. They had a terrific grantmaking agenda that included mentoring, mediation, alternative dispute resolution and much more. Yet they were puzzled as to why rates of violence were not going down. To an outsider it was obvious that their grantmaking agenda was just a small part of what was required to actually reduce rates of violence. A comprehensive strategy to reduce violence would include such things as community policing, gun control, supervised recreation for teens and broadly based efforts to address the causes of violence. The foundation had never actually taken the time to think about what such a comprehensive strategy would look like and how their grantmaking agenda fit within this strategy.

Figure 6.11 shows a special set of questions for Results Based Grantmaking. The questions are a variation on the questions presented in the Population and Performance Accountability chapters. Funders should start by deciding on the results they hope to affect in their grantee communities and what indicators would show whether those conditions are getting better or worse. How are the communities, cities or states now doing on the relevant population indicators? What is the story behind the baselines? Who are the partners who have a role to play in doing better? What would it take to do better? And what is our role in doing better?

A growing number of funders are now using RBA and Results Based Grantmaking methods. Many United Ways including the United Ways in Santa Cruz, California; Indianapolis, Indiana; Des Moines, Iowa; Louisville, Kentucky; Cincinnati, Ohio; Burlington, Vemont; Peel, Ontario and the Lehigh Valley in Pennsylvania have been using RBA for many years. The Foundation Consortium for California's Children and Youth has used RBA to plan and manage community change efforts on behalf of its twenty member foundations. The Annie E. Casey Foundation and its grantees have made extensive use of RBA and results-based grantmaking in planning and managing their agenda, including civic and neighborhood initiatives in Atlanta, Des Moines, Indianapolis, Louisville, Hartford, Milwaukee, Oakland, San Antonio and Seattle. The Gates Foundation and the Higherlife Foundation have used RBA to plan some of their international charitable work. And a number of federal grantmaking agencies have used RBA methods for strategic planning and grants management including several institutes in the National Institutes of Health, the Department of Education Promise Neighborhoods Initiative and the Health Resources and Services Administration, Bureau of Primary Health Care.

WHERE RESULTS-BASED ACCOUNTABILITY
THINKING HAS WORKED

Montgomery County, Ohio: Family and Children First Council[118]

Formed in 1996, the Family and Children First Council is the lead collaborative for health and human services in Montgomery County (Dayton), Ohio. Since 1998, the Council has published a series of annual *Reports to the Community on Outcomes and Indicators*. One of the indicators included in the report is the overall school attendance rate for the 16 school districts within the county.

Figure 6.12

The first report showed a downward trend in the percent of children attending school between the 1991/92 school year and the 1993/94 school year. This was followed by a further reduction in 1995/96. The 1995/96 rate of 90.5% was 2.6 percentage points below the state attendance rate for all schools. Between one and four school districts failed to meet the state's 93% standard in any given year during that time period and five failed to meet it in school year 1996/97. Attendance was clearly a problem, and it was getting worse.

After releasing the first report, the Council considered all of the published data, and chose three areas in which it could mobilize community responses: School Readiness and School Success, Alternative Learning Opportunities, and Family Violence. The school attendance indicator became a focus of the Alternative Learning Opportunities Initiative.

Each initiative was led by a champion, a respected community leader, who assembled a team of about 20 people with a stake in the problem. The Alternative Learning Opportunities Team (ALOT) brought together groups of local people who had diverse perspectives and experiences with this issue. They reviewed the data, and examined best practices from around the country.

[118.] Thanks to Bob Stoughton and the Montgomery County Family and Children First Council.

A key observation was that attendance was a problem all across the county, not just in the Dayton school district. Between the 1991/92 school year and the 1995/96 school year, attendance at 13 of the county's 16 school districts fell by an average of 1.6 points.

The team found it useful to think of three groups of young people: those who had already dropped out, those who were still in school and actively engaged, and those who were still in school but disengaged to the point where they could be considered "**in-school dropouts**." The team decided to focus on this last group, in part because there was already another community group working on the issue of dropouts.

There were two main elements in the ALOT team's plan. One element was the mentoring collaborative. It was created to coordinate and augment existing resources in the community, recruit, train and monitor mentors, and promote better matching of young people with mentors. Mentoring addresses some of the key characteristics of the target group: unhappy youth with serious discipline issues, often from single parent households.

The team launched the "Education - Think About It!" multimedia public education and outreach campaign. It was developed with focus groups of teens to make sure that the message, images, graphics, and music would capture the attention of the intended audience. The campaign called attention to the state's new truancy law and its provisions for holding parents and guardians more responsible for their child's attendance. It also advertised a local "one-stop" resource for dropouts and those at-risk of dropping out.

Since the ALOT team's work began in 1999, the overall county attendance rate has improved to 93.5% in school year 2003/2004. While the state's average attendance rate also improved during this period, the county rate improved twice as fast, closing the gap between them from 2.1% to 1.0%. The team cannot say with certainty what combination of actions and other factors caused the improvement, but the curve has turned and the trend is headed up.

Chapter 7:

IMPLEMENTATION ISSUES AND CHALLENGES
And stuff that didn't fit anywhere else

Bringing people together to do this work

There are many different ways to bring people together to do this work. Results-Based Accountability does not prescribe any particular method. Some groups are formed by law as in the case of the Family Connections Collaboratives in Georgia. Some are formed by executive order as in the case of the children's cabinets in Maryland and New Mexico. Some groups are formed as part of foundation initiatives. Others are spontaneous gatherings of people of like minds.

Almost all of these methods draw on the energy created by dissatisfaction. People who are not satisfied with their children's education may join together to work on school improvement. People not satisfied with community safety may join together to improve safety. People not satisfied with air and water quality may join together to work on the environment.

The sense that a situation has become intolerable is the most common reason that individuals and groups take action. In 1993, I was working in the Seattle area, and on a free day traveled to Anacortes, an old port north of the city. Anacortes has a large old boat that has been hauled onto shore and turned into a museum. It is the third in a series of "snag boats," specially designed to hoist dead trees out of the water. In 1888, there was a huge storm in the northwest that filled the Puget Sound with dead trees. Getting around by water was the most important means of transportation at the time, and the dead trees made navigation virtually impossible. This event caused so much difficulty that soon after, the US Congress appropriated $100,000 to build the first snag boat. This was a large sum of money at the time, particularly for a remote and undeveloped part of the country. The situation had become intolerable. People said in effect "This is not OK. We have to do something."

Mothers Against Drunk Driving was formed in 1980 by a group of women in California who thought our society's acceptance of drunk driving was intolerable. America joined World War II because the actions of Axis powers were intolerable. Those of us with leaking roofs often wait until the leak is intolerable before we call the roofer.

Can this sense of dissatisfaction be deliberately created? In Tillamook County, Oregon in 1990, the state report card on teen pregnancy rates spurred the formation of a group of leaders to take action. In 1993, the statistics on juvenile homicide in Boston spurred the creation of a broad partnership to take action. In the auto industry, data showing the U.S. losing market share to Japan spurred a new generation of cars and a new approach to management. There are countless examples.

One hypothesis of RBA is that data can be used deliberately to generate dissatisfaction and therefore action. Report cards on the well-being of children and families, or on community quality of life can make clear how bad the problems are. This might cause people to think that one or more of these conditions are intolerable, might lead people to say "That's not OK. We can do better." When Con Hogan was Secretary of Human Services in Vermont, he traveled around the state and presented local folks with the actual report card data on how children were doing in their community. On one such visit to Bennington, Vermont, he met with the local Rotary Club and some other members of the regional partnership. Con showed them two charts. The first showed that child abuse in Vermont had been going down in the last several years. The second chart showed that child abuse rates in Bennington were much higher than the state rate and getting worse. The people in the room were genuinely surprised and upset. After a couple of years of concerted effort, the Bennington numbers declined solidly toward the state averages. Numbers had created dissatisfaction and dissatisfaction brought people together to create change.

A better agenda for meetings

Ninety percent of the agenda in most meetings is taken up by people reporting on what they did since the last meeting. By the time this is finished, there is no time left for anything else. You go away and swear you are never going back to that meeting again, so next time you send a representative.

Imagine if the agenda were this:

1. **New data on the curves we are trying to turn.**
2. **New information on the story behind those curves.**
3. **New partners we need to bring to the table.**
4. **New information on what works.**
5. **New information on financing.**
6. **Changes to the action plan and budget.**
7. **Adjourn.**

This would be a different kind of meeting. It might last ten minutes or two hours, but it would be an action meeting, focused on how we're doing and what we need to do next. Save the "what I did last summer" material for a handout or the website. By going through this agenda you repeat the results thinking process each time you meet. Each time you do this, your action plan gets better. And new people who join the group will learn the turn the curve thinking process just by coming to the meetings.

The value and limits of data

RBA places a high value on the use of data. However, it is important to acknowledge that data is not the only source of knowledge about people, programs, agencies, and communities. There is, according to Star Trek's Data, an "ineffable" quality to human experience. Life is complex and cannot be reduced to a set of numbers and equations. This is why we place results and experience of results before any attempt to find measures. It is also why we report on progress using stories, anecdotes and accomplishments that go beyond the numbers.

But, as powerful as these other forms of knowledge may be, there is an unavoidable importance to data. In complex environments, it is often impossible to know if things are getting better or worse without data. There are some who argue for one extreme or the other, who value data too highly or not at all. The answer, like most answers, lies in between.

As a society, we lack regular reliable data on the well-being of children, families and communities. We are hundreds (or thousands) of years behind the business community which has always used data to track progress. Stock market data is now updated every second. We are 60 years behind the creation of reliable labor market data by the Bureau of Labor Statistics. We now take unemployment data and consumer price data for granted. We are at least 50 years behind public health data. The Centers for Disease Control and Prevention began tracking national health data in the early 1950's. It will take time to get the data we need. Perhaps one day, there will be a Bureau of Child, Family and Community Statistics with up-to-date data published each day in the newspaper next to statistics on the economy.

Creating data

If you don't have any good data, experience can be used as a temporary substitute to drive the decision-making process and create an action plan. But working without data is ultimately unsatisfying. Sooner or later you need data.

One way to get data is to create it. One of my favorite stories about creating data involves a senator from the Maryland State Legislature. Senator Bernie Fowler came from one of the counties on the eastern shore of the Chesapeake Bay. As a young man, Bernie went down to the Chesapeake to go crabbing. He would wade out into the water until it was up to his neck. The water was clear enough to see his feet and, of course, the crabs. As the years went by, the water in the Chesapeake Bay got dirtier and Bernie got angrier. One year, he decided to stage an event. He went down to his old boyhood crabbing spot and waded out into the water until he lost sight of his sneakers. The distance from the shore to this point became known as the Bernie Fowler Sneaker Test of Water Quality. The first year he did this, people thought he was crazy. By the third year, the secretary of the Environmental Protection Agency was wading into the water with

Bernie and the national television cameras were rolling. Bernie had created data on water quality.[119]

We have been intimidated by the high priests of the data community. We have been led to believe that unless data comes from a sophisticated computer system or a scientifically valid sample, it is no good. I am a great fan of high quality data when you can get it. But such data is not always available, and we need to be pragmatic.

Not all data must be created by experts. You can sometimes create your own data. Here are some simple examples of data collection that you might not find in any of the textbooks on the subject:

Take a walking tour of the neighborhood each month and count vacant houses or vacant lots. Plot your findings on a chart and watch the trend line.

At the monthly community meeting, ask, "How many people here know someone who was a victim of a crime in the last 30 days?" Count the percent of people who raise their hands. Plot this on a chart and use the baseline to drive thinking about actions you could take to improve community safety.

When I worked in state government, we often had to make policy judgments with little or no data to help us decide what to do. When this happened, we would sometimes send someone to one of the local departments of social services to read 20 case records and tell us what they found. We didn't have the time or money for a full research study. What we could get from reading 20 case records wasn't perfect, but it was a lot better than nothing. You can do the same.

Composite measures

A composite measure is created when different measures are combined to form a single measure. The most common type of composite measure is an index derived from combining, and sometimes weighting, other measures. The Consumer Price Index is one of the bestknown of these and is used to track rates of inflation. Consumer Reports Magazine uses an index to rate the quality of consumer products, US News and World Report rates "America's Best Hospitals," Governing Magazine uses an index to rate state, county and city governments, Money Magazine, Forbes and many other create indices to rate "the best places to live in the U.S."[120]

Indices can be powerful, but only if people understand what they mean. Some indices are so complex, they leave readers or community members confused or indifferent. Imagine

---

[119] The Trib Team Monitor, Winter/Spring 1998, No. 6, dnr.state.md.us/bay/tribstrat/monitor/WinSpring98.

[120] A Google search on "best places to live" produced over 13 million citations.

a school meeting where the principal presented parents with a "school success index." The principal would face blank stares and puzzled looks. It would be far better to talk about the handful of well-known component measures, such as the percent of students reading at grade level, the graduation rate, and the attendance rate. It is best to avoid complicated indices, and use well-understood or easy to explain measures instead.

There are, however, other cases where composite measures are an essential tool. State departments of education, for example, are responsible for reviewing all school districts in the state for compliance with special education program requirements. Reviewers must read hundreds of records, interview teachers and parents, and rate the compliance of each district on dozens of different requirements. The initial data set is extremely large. Composite measures can help to report these data in a coherent and comprehensible way. The agency can identify those local school districts that are in compliance with 90% or more of performance requirements. This huge data set is reduced to a single number, the percent of special education programs with 90% or higher compliance. This becomes a point on a baseline and a curve that can be turned toward 100%.

Emergency management is another area where composite measures are particularly useful. Natural disasters are unpredictable and unpreventable events. The most important indicators are not the rate that such disasters occur or the rates of death and destruction. The best measures are those that deal with preparedness. Preparedness, like the special education reviews, involve hundreds of separate dimensions. Composite measurement can reduce these dimensions to a handful of measures such as the percent of emergency response agencies that score 90% or higher on readiness assessments. Similar measures, addressing the timeliness and adequacy of the response, can be used to rate emergency management performance after an exercise or actual disaster.

Composite measures can also be useful where the purpose of the work is easy to define rhetorically, but hard to define operationally. Take for example the community and economic development initiatives designed to help turn "troubled neighborhoods" into "vibrant neighborhoods" or the United Nations economic assistance programs that seek to help under-developed countries to become "developed." To what extent is a neighborhood vibrant or a country developed?

Composite measurement methods can help make notions like vibrancy and development more concrete. The first step is to list all of the characteristics of a vibrant neighborhood or a developed country. Second, rate each characteristic on an appropriate scale from good to bad. Third, collapse these ratings into a single number by counting the percent of characteristics that rate in the highest categories.

We used this method with a large city community foundation that was working with low income neighborhoods to help them become "thriving neighborhoods." We listed all the possible characteristics of a thriving neighborhood, and then pared these down to the ten most important. The final list included population results such as *The Community is Safe, People Have Decent Housing, and There is a Strong Business and Shopping Sector.*

We then rated each characteristic using a two step process. For each characteristic we asked whether the conditions right now were "good" or "bad."[121] Each characteristic was marked "G" or "B" based on group consensus. Next we asked about the direction of change over the past two years; whether things were getting better, getting worse or about the same. Beside each letter we placed an arrow going up, down or sideways.

This method yields six possible scores. The two best categories were *good and getting better*, and *good and about the same*. The four troublesome categories were *good and getting worse, bad and getting better, bad and about the same* and *bad and getting worse*. We counted how many of the ten characteristics received the two best ratings. To everyone's surprise, six of the ten characteristics for this neighborhood were in the top two categories. We had given an operational definition to a "thriving neighborhood," and created a rough way to measure progress. This rating could be plotted as a point on a baseline and could be used to drive a turn the curve process. And a pathway to understanding the story behind this curve and potential actions was immediately evident in the four characteristics that rated in the four bad categories.

The relationship between Results-Based Accountability and evaluation

The word evaluation, like other words in this book, has many possible meanings. One definition of evaluation is a study of how well a program or strategy is working or has worked. Some evaluations are concerned with process, some with results, some with both. Some evaluations are full scale research projects and some are less formal information gathering and analysis.

Evaluation studies can provide information that is useful in both Population and Performance Accountability. Program evaluations provide data for baselines and information about the story behind the baselines. Managers and funders can use this information to help manage the program and make funding decisions. Evaluation reports that show a program is making a difference in the lives of its customers can be used to promote and defend the program in budget and political processes. Evaluation reports that reveal problems with a program's performance can help improve that performance.

In Population Accountability, evaluation plays two roles. When partners get to the "what works?" question, they need information about what has worked in other places. The evaluation literature can help identify programs that are effective and therefore deserve to be considered as part of the action plan. The second role for evaluation is the study of the population change process itself. Are the partners achieving what they set out to achieve? Are the curves turning? When evaluation is used in this way, it can become an accountability process, similar to RBA.

It is important to note that both Population and Performance Accountability methods in this book can be used with or without a formal evaluation. Managers and commu-

---

121.   You could use OK or not OK or some more refined scale.

nity partners can use RBA methods to do for themselves what evaluation companies are paid a lot of money to do, including gathering data, analyzing data and using data to improve performance.

The principal difficulty with evaluations is their cost. Evaluations can be very expensive, and not all programs can afford an evaluation. Most evaluations are done by outside organizations, usually only once in the life of a program or population initiative. These kind of evaluations may not help the organization build its own capacity for data collection and analysis after the evaluators leave. Evaluations sometimes collect more information than is needed to manage the program. Excessive data collection can become a burden that detracts from the program's performance. It is important to make sure the evaluation does not become more important than the program or initiative being evaluated.

There is a sizable industry in the United States devoted to producing evaluations. This industry appears to be divided into two armed camps. The first camp draws on the tradition of independent outside investigators. This sometimes means white coat evaluators who come in three years after the program is over to explain why it failed. The second kind of evaluation is self-evaluation or empowerment evaluation.[122] Evaluators from this camp create a partnership with the manager. The evaluation takes place during the life of the program, and the evaluator helps the manager interpret data and make mid-course corrections. RBA is completely aligned with this second approach to evaluation.

Evaluations often try to answer cause and effect questions about the relationship between program design and program results. These questions can be posed in terms of the connection between *How well did we do it?* and *Is anyone better off?* measures, and the four quadrant method of identifying performance measures has been useful in designing evaluation studies. Evaluations using control groups can sometimes provide answers about what program design leads to the best customer results. However, control group research is the most expensive of all evaluations and it is not always financially feasible or ethically permissible. The matter of establishing cause and effect relationships in complex environments, in the absence of control group research, is the subject of the next section.

Demonstrating contribution to community change

Has your program ever been asked to **prove** its impact on the community? Most funders demand this of their grantees. And many evaluators try to oblige. The problem is that it is the **wrong question**. There are two things wrong with this question. First, it is extremely rare that one program by itself can turn a curve at the population level. It usually takes a set of actions by many partners to do this. Programs should never be held responsible, by themselves, for producing change in population conditions.

---

[122].　See the works of Dr. David Fetterman at Stanford University, Dr. Lynn Usher at the University of North Carolina and Dr. Susan Brutschy at Applied Survey Research in Santa Cruz, California.

Secondly, chaos and complexity theory teaches us that precise cause and effect relationships in complex environments are not just difficult to know, they're impossible to know.

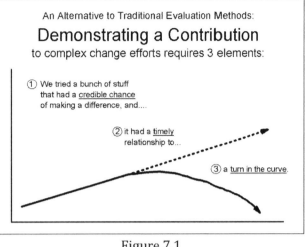

Figure 7.1

What part of the reduction in alcohol related traffic fatalities was caused by Mothers Against Drunk Driving? How much did the mentoring component of Boston's strategy reduce the juvenile homicide rate? How much does the help you provide your children with their homework contribute to their grades in school? We can't know the extent to which a program impacts population conditions and we need to stop pretending that we can.

We can, however, ask whether an **entire strategy** has had an effect on population conditions. This is a question of a different order of magnitude. Here we seek to know, not the contribution of any one program or component, but the effect of a **set** of actions. The evaluation community has been slow to provide methods to deal with this challenge. The methods of control group research do not apply to complex environments where variables cannot be controlled.

Here's a way to do it. You can demonstrate that a collection of actions made a contribution to community change if you have three pieces of evidence:

1. You tried a bunch of **stuff that had a credible chance of making a difference, and**
2. You saw a **timely relationship to a...**
3. **Turn in the curve.**

All three elements must be present to show contribution. Take one away and the case collapses.

Here's an example. Figure 7.2 shows foster care (UK: looked after children) caseloads and costs in Maryland from 1972 to 1986. The dark line headed down from left to right is the total foster care caseload in Maryland. The dark line headed up from left to right is the cost of the foster care program in state general funds. Through 1980, the caseload was trending down and cost was trending up as shown by the lines marked "trend." Beginning in 1980, the Department of Human Resources implemented an extensive set of reforms designed to keep children safely with their biological parents and out of foster care. The Department implemented one of the first family preservation programs in the United States, reduced caseload ratios for workers in foster care and protective services, provided in-home aides as backup support to child welfare workers, implemented a foster care review board system, and many other changes. In total, these investments cost approximately $16.2 million in state general funds between FY 1980 and FY 1986.

Beginning in 1980, we saw a marked divergence from the trendline. By 1986, the cumulative difference between the trend and actual caseloads was 11,400 child-years in foster care! The difference between trend and actual costs was approximately $24.2 million in combined direct savings and cost avoidance, a return on investment of $1.50 for each dollar expended. All three elements were present. We tried a bunch of stuff that had a credible chance of making a difference, and we saw a timely turn in both the caseload and cost curves.

This kind of demonstration is pretty much the best you are ever going to achieve in complex environments. This picture represents, not proof of causality, but **circumstantial evidence** that what we did **contributed** to the change. This approach comes from the budget world, not the research world. Researchers may discount this approach as not rigorous enough,

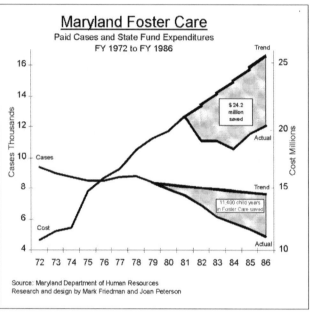

Figure 7.2

with no control for external variables. In the real world of budgeting, however, this method of demonstrating effect has been used explicitly or implicitly for decades. When it is done well, it carries a lot of weight with policy makers and can help win recognition for successful initiatives and the resources to continue the work. It is time for funders to recognize this method as a legitimate way to evaluate complex change processes.

There is a **fourth** criterion that can be added to the basic three. The case for contribution is even more powerful if you can also show that the curve turned in a direction counter to a background trend, such as a comparable trend for the rest of the city, county, state or nation. In the foster care example, this fourth criterion is also present because the actual national foster care caseload tracked along a path almost identical to the state trendline. The Maryland caseload declined faster than the rest of the country.[123]

---

123. Thanks to Bob Pillsbury, David Murphey and Con Hogan for their contributions to developing these criteria.

It will not have escaped your attention that the Maryland foster care example is about program performance, and not population or community change. The same method can be used to for both population change processes and for the performance of programs, agencies and service systems. It is no less of a challenge to demonstrate that a program contributed to positive changes in its customers' lives. In the fractal that is sociology and biology, organizations and human beings are as complex as communities.

Finally, these methods can be used to estimate the effects of **prevention** programs. The classic challenge in assessing prevention programs is estimating the extent to which something **didn't** happen. You can't roll the clock back and see what happens without the program. How many teen pregnancies were avoided in Tillamook County? How many juvenile homicides were avoided in Boston? If a baseline with a credible forecast can be established, then the difference between the actual and forecasted values can be used to estimate the prevention effect. Actuaries in insurance companies do this all the time. They forecast your life expectancy based on historical data for people like you. They decide what kind of gamble the company should make on how healthy you will be and how long you will live. If you need to estimate prevention benefits for a program, consider asking for help from an insurance company.

Cost benefit ratios and return on investment

Cost benefit ratios and return on investment rates are among the most important of all financial measures. While these rates are relatively easy to calculate for business enterprises, they can be extremely difficult to calculate for government and non-profit organizations. The reason is that the "benefit" part of the equation cannot be readily computed for most programs that have no financial bottom line.

There are, of course, some government programs that do have a financial bottom line, like child support enforcement, tax collection and other services that handle money. For child support enforcement and tax collection, it is possible to calculate the total amount collected per dollar expended. Audit functions also lend themselves to the determination of financial benefit by calculating the saved or avoided costs associated with audit findings compared to audit costs.

For non-financial programs, the methods required to estimate financial benefits are much more complicated. There are two basic approaches. The first and simpler method involves comparing the program's success rate with its customers versus data for the general public, and attributing a value to the difference. For example, a program that works with teens can compare the rate of teen pregnancies for young women in the program to the rate for the community as a whole. The difference represents an estimate of teen pregnancies that have been prevented. This estimate can be combined with separate estimates of the social costs for each teen pregnancy. One study, for example, found that the average adolescent mother receives welfare and food stamp benefits valued at $1,400 per year for the first 13 years of parenthood.[124] The total bene-fit of the program can be calculated by multiplying the number of avoided pregnancies by the cost per pregnancy. There are challenges at each stage of this calculation, but this method has produced usable estimates.[125]

I completed this type of analysis for an article I coauthored with Dr. C. Patrick Chaulk and Richard Dunning about Direct Observed Therapy (DOT). DOT is a treatment ap-proach for tuberculosis designed to address the difficulty of getting patients to take a complex regimen of medications on an exact schedule. Effective DOT involves building a treatment plan with the patient and using paid public health nurses, or unpaid trained volunteers to actually observe the patient taking the medicine. In 1978, the Baltimore City Health Department was one of the first in the country to adopt DOT, and tuberculosis rates showed a significant decline soon after. But there was continu-ing controversy about whether the extra costs of DOT were justified. With our analy-sis, we showed that implementation of DOT in Baltimore produced an estimated net savings of $25.9 to $27.1 million dollars between 1978 and 1992.[126] We compared the actual tuberculosis rates for Baltimore during this period to the rates that would have existed had Baltimore continued to follow the same path as other large cities in the US. The difference between these rates, combined with the average treatment cost per case, allowed us to estimate total savings from avoided tuberculosis cases in Baltimore. The avoided treatment cost could then be compared to the additional cost of DOT treat-ment. This analysis has helped convince people in the treatment community that the extra cost of DOT is justified by the avoided costs associated with prevented cases of tuberculosis.

There is an alternative method for calculating cost benefit that is more complicated but also more thorough. This method starts by inventorying all the possible places where the benefits of a program potentially show up in the expenditures of govern-ment and non-governmental organizations. The program's effects are then estimated for each weekly or monthly cohort of clients moving through the program. Using stud-ies where possible, and informed estimates where studies are not available, it is pos-sible to calculate the rates at which each cohort of clients produces savings in other parts of the system. The benefits for an individual cohort can be calculated over a time period of typically 5 to 20 years. By simulating the rate at which cohorts enter the pro-gram, the total costs and benefits can be calculated over time.

In an unpublished FPSI study, this approach to cost benefit modeling was used to an-alyze an innovative drug seller diversion program in San Francisco called Street to

---

124. Kids Having Kids: A Robin Hood Foundation Special Report on the Costs of Adolescent Childbearing, Maynard, Rebecca A. (Ed.), 1996, p. 52.

125. See the section on "Is my program working?" in Chapter 4.

126. "Revisiting supervised therapy: Modeling the epidemiology and costs of directly observed therapy in Baltimore," C. Patrick Chaulk, M.D. M.P.H., Mark Friedman, Richard Dunning, MSW, 1999.

Work. The program dropped the charges against first time drug sellers if they successfully completed a job training and placement program. The analysis compared costs associated with traditional handling of cases to the alternative pathways likely under the new program. The analysis showed an estimated 3.5 to 1 return on investment over four years in the justice system, and a 4.2 to 1 return when tax and social service systems were included.

Calculating cost benefit ratios for non-financial programs is a complex and time consuming undertaking, but it can provide powerful arguments for additional investments in successful programs. It is almost always true that the costs of prevention show up in one part of the budget and the savings show up in another. Cost benefit analyses can link the two and help place prevention programs on a more sound financial footing.

Using Results-Based Accountability for individual customers and your own personal life.

A teacher in one of my workshops came up to me and said, "You know this method could be used to track the performance of the students in my class." Several months later, another workshop participant told me that he had used RBA methods to manage the disciplinary problems he was having with his son, and it worked. Others have told me they've used RBA in making decisions about their personal lives. And, a few years ago, I used these methods to lose weight.

Let's look at how RBA would work for tracking a child's performance in school. There is a reading test for elementary school children (DIBELS) where the child reads a paragraph out loud and the teacher scores the total number of words read correctly. It is a simple test that can be applied periodically throughout the year. For each child, the teacher would keep a graph of the scores on this test over time. The teacher would compare the child's progress with class progress, consider what might be causing any lack of progress, consider partners with a role to play and craft a plan to help the child improve.

Let's see how it would work for dieting. Weigh yourself every morning and keep a graph of these numbers. Draw a horizontal goal line across the graph at your desired weight. Consider the story behind this baseline. What is causing you to weigh more than you want? Who are the partners who can help you do better? What could work to do better? What do you propose to do? What specific version of changed diet and exercise will work for you? Implement your action plan and watch to see if the curve turns. Repeat the thinking process until you cross the goal line. The short book "Results Based Dieting" describes this method in more detail.

There are countless other applications. The same process used to change programs and communities can also be used to change your life.

Comparing frameworks

Framework names seem to lay an exclusive claim to certain ideas. The Balanced Scorecard is the balanced framework. The Logic Model is the logical framework. RBA is the framework concerned with results. Nonsense. All three approaches are balanced, logical and concerned with results. The comparison of frameworks has nothing to do with the framework's name.

Instead, frameworks can be compared in two ways: in terms of their structure and in terms of their utility and ease of use.[127] Let's look at the structural differences between frameworks first.

Comparing Structure: It is possible to crosswalk or compare the components of one framework to the corresponding components of another framework. Most frameworks are trying to do essentially the same thing but differ in how they label and sequence ideas. The Crosswalk Tool in Figure 7.3 (and Appendix D) allows the structure of RBA to be compared to the structure of any other framework. This, in turn, enables any two frameworks to be compared to each other.

The Crosswalk tool shows RBA down the left side of the page. The Population Accountability progression is shown first: from population to results, indicators, experience, baselines, story behind the baselines, partners, what works, and an action plan. The Performance Account-

Framework Crosswalk		
Population Accountability	_Example_	Logic Model (framework name)
1. Population		
2. Results		5. Goal
3. Indicators		
Data Development Agenda		
4. Baselines		
5. Story behind the baselines		
Info/Research Agenda (causes)		
6. Partners		
7. What works		
Info/Research Agenda (solutions)		
8. Action Plan		
9. Budget		
Performance Accountability		
1. Customers		
2. Performance measures		
How much did we do?		3. Output
How well did we do it?		
Is anyone better off?		4. Outcome
Data Development Agenda		
3. Baselines		
4. Story behind the baselines		
Info/Research Agenda (causes)		
5. Partners		
6. What works		
Program actions		2. Activity
Partner's actions		
Info/Research Agenda (solutions)		
7. Action Plan		
8. Budget		1. Input

Figure 7.3

ability progression is shown next, starting with customers, performance measures, baselines, story behind the baselines, partners, what works, and an action plan.[128]

---

127.   The Rennsalaerville Institute (TRI), and authors Bob Penna and Bill Phillips, have done a nice job of comparing both the structure and the strengths and weaknesses of nine "outcome" frameworks in their book "Outcome Frameworks, An Overview for Practitioners," available from TRI or Amazon.com.

128.   This also serves as a very neat compact summary of the RBA framework.

The comparison framework is shown in the right column with each element listed across from its RBA counterpart. The elements of the comparison framework are numbered to show the typical sequencing of ideas and how that sequencing differs from RBA. [129] The middle column provides space for examples that illustrate how the terms are used in the comparison framework.

The crosswalk tool makes it possible to see how other frameworks label the same idea with different words, combine two or more ideas under a single word, or place the elements of the framework in a different order.

The right column of Figure 7.3 shows the cross walk between RBA and a typical logic model framework.[130] Notice that the natural sequence of steps in RBA works down the page. And the typical logic model sequence works up the page. So RBA starts with population or customer results and works towards an action plan. The logic model progression starts with program inputs and works towards customer outcomes and population "goals." This comparison shows that the word "outcome" in most logic models closely corresponds to the idea of "customer result" or "customer outcome" in RBA.

The crosswalk allows you to see gaps in the structure of this particular logic model. For example, there is nothing in this logic model progression that corresponds to the *How well did we do it?* measures. You can also see that this version of the logic model has no separate treatment of Population Accountability and presents Population Accountability as a linear extension of Performance Accountability. This is typical of frameworks designed for program performance that do not address the non-linear relationship between Population and Performance Accountability.

Comparing utility and ease of use: The Crosswalk Tool, however, does not address comparisons of utility and ease of use. Such comparisons are difficult to create. There are no Consumer Reports analyses of frameworks, no framework showrooms, and no test drives. Like anything else, a framework can look good on paper, but how does it perform on the road?

There are two ways in which the utility and ease of use of frameworks could be compared. A research study could be conducted to analyze which frameworks have the best track record. Which frameworks are most successful at actually improving community and customer results? In what percent of cases is there a good turn the curve story to tell? To what extent do partners attribute success to the use of a particular framework?

---

129. Remember that, except for placing the story before what works, RBA is not necessarily linear. The steps can be done in any order as long as you do them all. The Crosswalk Tool shows the most common sequencing of each framework.

130. This version of the logic model is taken from the first round of publications on this subject by the United Way of America.

The second method would measure customer satisfaction.[131] Which frameworks are easiest to use or best liked by framework "customers?" How easy or hard are the frameworks to implement? How much training and on-going support from consultants is required? Is the framework adaptable to different parts of the organization or different community efforts? How much does it cost to implement and use the framework?

Unfortunately, none of these comparisons have been done systematically. Decisions are often made on the basis of who knows the boss, what the boss happens to see at a conference, read in a book, or find on the internet. Indeed, RBA has benefited from all of these methods. However, these kind of selection processes are not in the best interest of the purchasing organizations or the field of accountability itself. The constant churning that goes with adopting and abandoning systems is expensive and fuels the cynical view that all frameworks are the same and none of them work very well.[132]

One defense against this problem is to go into the marketplace armed with a set of criteria against which to judge the different framework choices. We all bring such criteria, explicitly or implicitly, to every other purchasing decision. A good set of criteria to use is the one we started with at the beginning of the book: Simple, Common Sense, Plain Language, Minimum Paper, Useful.

I believe that RBA holds up well against these criteria. Most people find RBA to be a common sense approach that can be quickly applied to their work. RBA makes use of plain language and simple formats. All of the materials are free for use by public and non-profit organizations.[133] And organizations are encouraged to develop their own capacity to support implementation, and become independent of consultants.

Comparing Results-Based Accountability to Logic Models: Logic models are perhaps the most widely used accountability framework in the US. Most logic models are designed for Performance Accountability and do not address Population Accountability or do so in a very limited way. RBA and logic models differ significantly in their starting points. Logic models start with a program or proposed action and identify a series of causes and effects that lead to customer and/or population results. RBA starts with one or more results and identifies a set of proposed actions to improve those results.

Starting with programs and testing the logic of their contribution to results can be a useful thing to do. It is in fact something that partners naturally do when considering "what works" in the RBA framework. The question, "Why do you think that will work?" leads to a logic model or "theory of change" response. But logic models are insufficient

---

131. Physician heal thyself.
132. This partly explains why there have been so many fads running through this field over the last century.
133. And small for-profit consulting firms. See the notices following Chapter 9.

as the overarching planning framework, because they start in the wrong place, with programs and not results.[134] Much of logic model work grows out of the old way of thinking that is program-centric, assuming that programs are the solution. RBA starts with the results, the end conditions we hope to achieve, and works backwards to strategies to do this. This leads to a much larger and richer set of solutions than just programs, including a broad array of partner contributions and no-cost and low-cost ideas. Jolie Bain Pillsbury has a nice way of describing this difference as a Copernican revolution in social policy. We once thought that results revolved around programs at the center. We now know that programs revolve around results at the center.

Some versions of logic models are very complicated, tedious and time consuming. I have encountered people who say they have been working on their logic models for months and even years.[135] Ask the people who advocate the use of logic models if they have ever completed a logic model for their own operation. There is a very good chance they haven't. Ask them why and they will say "Because we know how our program is supposed to work." And that's the point. You also know how your program is supposed to work. Logic models seem to start with the assumption that managers must analyze their program's operation in great detail in order to identify performance measures. In the end, this simply wastes a lot of time. You can get to roughly the same place using RBA methods in about an hour (See Appendix G). Most managers admit that logic models themselves have little utility as a management tool. And most people exposed to both logic models and RBA find the latter much easier to understand and much more useful.

However, the logic model industry in the US is so large, with so many vested interests, that critiques of its efficacy are hard to find. While we wait for the systematic comparisons of utility and ease of use, recommended above, RBA poses an alternative to logic models and other frameworks that are not serving the needs of managers or community partners.

[134.] Some people will argue that logic models start with results and then circle back to describe how a program contributes to results. Same difference.

[135.] In one state that shall go unnamed, they produced a logic model for just a portion of the human services agency that, when finished, covered so many pages it had to be taped together and read with a magnifying glass. (I'm not making this up.) Another logic model was reported to cover an entire conference table, with many of the pathways leading to a box that said "See Vivian."

WHERE RESULTS-BASED ACCOUNTABILITY THINKING HAS WORKED

Santa Cruz County, California[136]

In Santa Cruz County, California, the United Way, the Dominican Hospital and many other community based organizations have jointly sponsored a quality of life report card, known as the Community Assessment Project (CAP). The project has been managed by Applied Survey Research (ASR), a non-profit research and evaluation company based in Santa Cruz County. ASR has collected data for over 120 indicators for the economy, education, health, public safety, the social environment, and the natural environment and has conducted an annual telephone survey with county residents. The CAP report card has provided data that has galvanized the county into action for children and families.

The first CAP report in 1995 showed alarming rates of youth in the 9th and 11th grades who self-reported using marijuana and alcohol in the last 30 days. Data revealed that in 1994, 51% of Santa Cruz County 9th graders and 55% of 11th

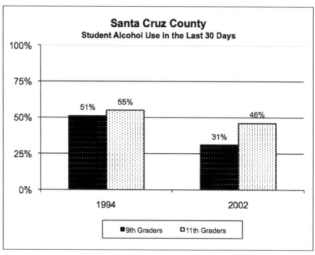

Figure 7.4

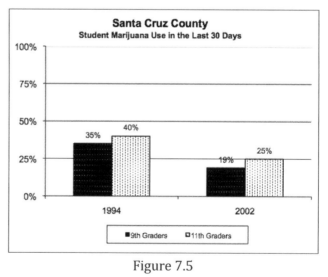

Figure 7.5

---

136.   Thanks to the partners in Santa Cruz County. For a picture of the Santa Cruz data and more information click on: whatworks-scruz.org/pdf_files/ds_youth_alc.pdf

graders reported using alcohol in the last thirty days. For marijuana use, 35% percent of Santa Cruz County 9th graders and 40% of 11th graders reported using the drug in the last month.

Following release of the first CAP report, a coalition of 110 agencies, organizations and individuals came together to combat drug and alcohol use among youth. The group identified five outcomes and developed seven strategies, including new alcohol laws, public education programs, a grand jury report, youth leadership training, home visiting programs, and linkages to other initiatives for youth. A countywide panel on youth access to alcohol developed policy recommendations for schools, law enforcement, land use / zoning, and businesses. Since 1997, over $1 million has been raised for support activities devoted to teens, including two new teen centers and two new teen residential treatment centers.

The CAP report, issued in 2003, showed a significant decline in the use of both substances in both grades. From 1994 to 2002, alcohol use by Santa Cruz County 9th graders was down 20%, as compared to overall California 9th graders who experienced a 10% decline. For marijuana use, Santa Cruz County 9th graders showed a 16% drop from 1994 to 2002, as compared to a 10% drop for California 9th graders. Marijuana use was down 15% for Santa Cruz County 11th graders, and only 3% for California 11th graders. Community leaders credit the public/private partnership strategies and the use of RBA methods as important contributors to turning these curves.

Chapter 8:

CLOSING

Results change everything

An agency executive told me that his whole staff shifted their thinking from checking compliance to helping programs succeed. A front line worker told me this is the first time in her career she and her colleagues have talked with each other about whether their customers were better off. A businessman told me this is the first time any discussion of social change has ever made sense to him. When people focus on the well-being of communities and customers, they reconnect to the reasons they became teachers, social workers, doctors, nurses, and police officers. They remember why they ran for elected office or why they gave up their nights and weekends to join with their neighbors to work for a better community. Results provide a common purpose that brings people together. Results can transform processes characterized by blame, conflict, competition, and inaction into processes where people see what they share in common and how working together is in everyone's interest. When so many things divide us - race, class, ethnicity, religion, politics and money - results have a power to unite us. This does not make the challenge of improving communities and programs any easier. But it can restore peoples' hope about what is possible. And it can lead to the kind of solutions that can only come from a diverse group of partners working together.

What if 1,000 communities turned a curve?

Imagine if 1,000 communities created a turn the curve table. Imagine if they actually turned a curve and measurably improved the quality of life for the people of that community!

One of the premises of Results-Based Accountability is that, while money is important, it is less powerful than the combined energy of the people and other assets in communities.[137] When that energy is focused in a disciplined way, almost anything can be accomplished. We do not need to wait for new money to be available to see a revolution in communities across the country.

Communities can begin to turn around quality of life conditions with the resources they already have. What stands in the way is not the possibility of change but the belief in that possibility and the methods to make it real.

One major reason for lack of belief is that past methods have failed us. The single most common reason why people leave community work or fail to join in the first place is

---

[137.] See the excellent work of John McKnight and others on assets-based planning.

disillusionment with past efforts that were all talk and no action. Another common reason is the psychology of dependence that suggests that government will take care of us, and if it doesn't, then there's nothing much we can do. If there is a method that is not all-talk-no action, that can produce meaningful action without higher level sanction or support, then these excuses dissolve. RBA is such a method.

There are many communities that have already embraced this possibility and acted to turn one or more curves. If 1,000 more communities took on the challenge, there could be a change of sufficient scope to represent a true transformation of community life, and a noticeable improvement in the well-being of children and families across the country.

The leadership for these efforts cannot come from one source. We have seen leadership from many places, from government sponsored collaboratives to private citizens meeting in the back of a restaurant. But every community has the seeds of leadership that can grow into significant change.

What if 1,000 agencies turned a curve?

We all interact with public and private sector agencies: the doctor's office, the health clinic, the school, the community college, and eventually Social Security. We all have complaints about how we were treated and ideas about how they could get better. What if they really did get better?

In the private for-profit sector, services get better because quality of service affects the bottom line. This is not a perfect system. It has brought us better cars and computers and also business scandals and air pollution. But profit is a powerful motivator for improved performance.

In public and non-profit services, customer results are the equivalent of profit. If we can observe it, we can measure it. And if we can measure it, we can improve it. Public and non-profit services can improve their performance using the Performance Accountability methods in this book. Since we all depend on these services, these improvements mean better lives for us and our children.

One thousand agencies is just 20 per state. What if 20 under-performing agencies in each state got serious about performance? Not just as a way to make their funders happy or look good before the legislature or city council, but with an earnest devotion to the lives of their customers. Those customers are us. The ripple effects of their improvement efforts would be noticeable in our lives and our communities. Why not declare that your agency will become one of the thousand and get started?

Conclusion

We stand at an historic juncture. Conclusions always start with this kind of statement because we are always at an historic juncture. The future hinges on what we do or fail to do today. In spite of all the great work being done, there are still many important things that we are mostly failing to do.

We are failing to invest in children and families before problems occur. We are failing to communicate in clear, plain language. We are failing to produce the data we need. We are failing to use the data we have. We are failing to use simple, common sense methods to manage programs and organize community change processes. We are failing to turn the curve on the most important measures of child, family and community well-being.

This book provides one possible approach to turning this around. What are the essential lessons of RBA? First, we must be able to talk to each other. Language discipline is necessary to any successful enterprise. The particular language discipline we need must distinguish between Population and Performance Accountability, and between ends and means. These distinctions can be found in the language discipline of results, indicators and performance measures, and in the three performance measurement categories *How much did we do? How well did we do it?* and *Is anyone better off?*

We must move from talk to action quickly. The RBA thinking process allows community partners and program managers to clarify their most important purposes, set measures that tell if these purposes are being met, and take action.

We must end the tyranny of too much paper and too much blame. Paper processes that burden managers and workers must be replaced with tools that are simple, powerful and most of all useful. We must stop using arbitrary performance targets to punish people, and instead move to a fair way to assess and credit progress using baselines. We must stop holding programs responsible for producing community impact and instead shift to crediting programs for their contributions to communities based on the changes they make in the lives of their customers.

Finally, we must not be satisfied with trying hard and hoping for the best. RBA is about producing measurable improvements for customers and communities. We must test ourselves using the discipline of data. If we try hard but none of the important numbers change, then something is wrong. We are either doing the wrong things or not enough of the right things. We must have a continuous improvement process that allows us to make mistakes, to learn, and to get better.

It is easy to find reams of rhetoric about these challenges. In RBA we show exactly how it can be done. There are tools, techniques and exercises to get on with the work and more are available on the websites raguide.org and resultsaccountability.com. They provide the discipline that passionate people need to be successful.

The RBA framework has evolved and will continue to evolve. I hope that others will feel it is worth their while to make contributions to our understanding of how these methods have worked and can work. There is a large and growing worldwide community of practitioners with implementation know-how and success stories to tell. I invite you to begin using RBA and become part of this community.

Chapter 9:

Virtual Chapter: The Websites

Results-Based Accountability is supported by two websites:

raguide.org

This website is an implementation guide for RBA, created with the support of the Annie E. Casey Foundation, the Foundation Consortium for California's Children and Youth, the Finance Project, the Colorado Foundation, and the Nebraska Children and Families Foundation. It provides answers to over 50 commonly asked questions about RBA, and includes over 100 tools, exercises, forms, formats, and other resources.

resultsaccountability.com

This is the website of the Fiscal Policy Studies Institute. It provides links to many papers on RBA and related topics, as well as links to other important resources. The website also is home to some other less serious work, including humorous essays on travel and other topics.

facebook.com/groups/RBAOBA

The Results-Based Accountability Facebook Group connects RBA/OBA experts and practitioners from around the world. Learn about what's happening in the RBA/OBA community. Share your work, your ideas and your questions. And keep up to date on the latest events and materials. The group is non-political and open to all.

EPILOGUE: On the Edge...

My early training and career interests involved mathematics and physics. I wandered into government largely because, in the late 1960's, matters of social justice seemed to be more interesting and important than finding the next smallest subatomic particle. But I have had a lifelong interest in the advancement of scientific thought that helps explain how the physical universe works. I believe that there is a small way in which Results-Based Accountability makes a contribution to understanding how the social universe works.

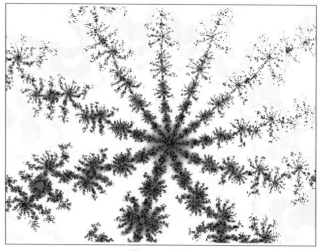

Figure 7.6

The distinction between Population and Performance Accountability reflects an underlying truth about the way societies and processes of social change are structured. RBA is a framework that clearly and completely explains the differences and connections between these two forms of accountability. While public and private organizations bear responsibility for their own performance, no organization can claim ownership of the well-being of a whole population. Population Accountability is not an extension of Performance Accountability but a separate, and perpetually unfinished, collective enterprise.

The RBA progression of thought from results to experience, measures, baselines, story, partners, what works and action can be applied to any population challenge from the highest level consideration of world peace to the economic prosperity of nations and states to the safety of children in a particular community. The same thought progression can be applied to any Performance Accountability challenge from the management of whole governments to large public and private sector agencies to the smallest program and finally to our personal lives. RBA may be the only planning framework of this scope.

The RBA thinking process is arguably an underlying archetype that connects and unifies business planning models, public health planning models and other data-driven decision making models. When RBA is used for public health planning it looks and feels like traditional public health planning. When it is used for business planning it looks and feels like business planning. The components of these other models can be mapped back to the components of RBA. This suggests that RBA is a simpler, more generic form of decision making reflective of what these models have in common.

Finally, one of the greatest mathematical, and in some respects philosophical, advances of our time has been the discovery of Chaos and Complexity Theory. It is possible to view social structures through this lens and see government bureaucracies and social networks as fractal entities with similar characteristics and structures at progressively larger and smaller levels of magnification. The world order in this view is not one of clockwork mechanics, but rather overlapping chaotic systems where cause and effect relationships are often impossible to understand. In a chaotic world, planning processes based on mechanical notions of cause and effect - this input leads to that output leads to that community change - don't work very well. Planning processes that are difficult to understand and implement make matters worse. If the planning process is complex and the content of the process is also complex, then the difficulty of the work grows exponentially. What is needed is a simple process, not dependent on rigid notions of causality, that can adapt to the fractal world, and contain the complex content of organizational and social change. RBA is such a process.

Notices regarding the use of Results-Based Accountability™ (RBA) material:

A note about use of the trademark symbol. The purpose of using the trademark symbol for Results-Based Accountability™ and Outcomes Based Accountability™ is to protect against those (thankfully) rare instances where these names are misused. It is not intended to compromise the free use of RBA by government and nonprofit/NGO organizations. As a general rule, the ™ symbol needs to be used only once in a document, after which the names may be used without the symbol. Where use of the symbol is likely to be misinterpreted as restricting the use of proprietary material, it may be omitted. Note that the acronyms RBA and OBA are not copyrighted and no trademark symbol should be used. RBA, for example, also stands for the Royal Bank of Australia and the Retail Bakers Association.

APPENDICES

A. Results-Based Accountability Implementation - Self Assessment Questions

B. Tool for Choosing a Common Language

C. How Other Planning Terminology Fits with Results-Based Accountability

D. Crosswalk Tool

E. Population and Performance Turn the Curve Exercises

F. Synopsis of Other Results-Based Accountability Exercises

G. A 5-step method for identifying performance measures for any program in about 45 minutes

H. More Performance Measurement Examples

I. Financing Self Assessment Questionnaire

J. Readings and Resources

Appendix A

RESULTS-BASED ACCOUNTABILITY IMPLEMENTATION

Self Assessment Questions

1. Has your group or organization adopted a common language using the Tool for Choosing a Common Language (Appendix B) or some other method? Does this common language allow you to clearly distinguish between Population and Performance Accountability? Between ends and means?

2. Has your organization identified one or more population level results or conditions of well-being stated in plain language to which your work contributes?

   a. Have you identified the 3 to 5 most important indicators for each of these results?

   b. Have you created a baseline with history and a forecast for each of these measures?

   c. Have you analyzed the story and causes behind these baselines?

   d. Do you have a written analysis of what it would take to turn these conditions around at the national, state, county, city or community level?

   e. Have you articulated the role your organization plays in such a strategy?

3. Has your organization established the 3 to 5 most important performance measures for what you do, using the Performance Accountability categories *How much did we do? How well did we do it? Is anyone better off?*

   a. Have you created a baseline with history and forecast for each of these measures?

   b. Do you track these measures on a daily, weekly, monthly or quarterly basis?

   c. Do you periodically review how you are doing on these measures, identify partners, and develop action plans to do better using the Performance Accountability 7 questions?

   d. Have you adapted your organization's management, budget, strategic planning, grant application, and progress reporting forms and formats to reflect systematic thinking about your contribution to population conditions and your organization's performance?

4. Are the population and performance baseline curves you are trying to turn displayed prominently as one or more charts on the wall?

5. Have you identified an in-house expert to train and coach other staff in this work?

6. Have you turned any curves?

A more complete Self Assessment Questionnaire with scoring instructions can be found at resultsaccountability.com/publications.

Appendix B

TOOL FOR CHOOSING A COMMON LANGUAGE

Ideas	Possible Labels (and modifiers)	Choice
A. THE BASICS		
1. A system or process for holding people in a geographic area responsible for the well-being of the total population or a defined subpopulation.	Population Accountability	
2. A system or process for holding managers and workers responsible for the performance of their programs, agencies and service systems.	Performance Accountability	
3. A condition of well-being for children, adults, families and communities.	Result, Outcome, Goal (Population, Community-wide)	
4. A measure that helps quantify the achievement of a population result.	Indicator, Benchmark (Population, Community-wide)	
5. A measure of how well a program, agency or service system is working.	Performance measure, Performance indicator	
6. A measure of the quantity of effort (how much service was delivered).	How much did we do?, Quantity of effort, Inputs, Outputs	
7. A measure of the quality of effort (how well the service functions were performed).	How well did we do it?, Quality of effort, Efficiency measure, Process measure	
8. A measure of the quantity and quality of effect on customers' lives. (Note: for infrastructure, effect on condition of infrastructure.)	Is anyone better off?, Is anyone or anything improved?, Customer result or outcome, Quantity & Quality of effect	
9. A visual display of the history and forecast(s) for a measure.	Baseline, Trendline	
10. Doing better than the forecast part of the baseline.	Turning the curve, Beating the baseline	

TOOL FOR CHOOSING A COMMON LANGUAGE (continued)

Ideas	Possible Labels (and modifiers)	Choice
B. OTHER IMPORTANT IDEAS		
1. A picture of a desired future that is hard but possible to attain.	Vision, Desired future	
2. The purpose of an organization.	Mission, Purpose	
3. A person (organization or entity) who directly benefits from service delivery. (generic category)	Customer, Client, Consumer, Beneficiary, Service user	
4. A person (or organization) with a significant interest in the performance of a program, agency or service system or population quality of life effort.	Stakeholder, Constituent	
5. A person (or organization) with a role to play in achieving desired ends.	Partner (Current, Potential, Active, Inactive)	
6. An analysis of causes and conditions that helps explain why a baseline looks the way it does.	Story behind the baseline, Root cause analysis	
7. Possible actions that could have a positive effect on a population indicator or performance measure.	What works, Options	
8. A coherent set of actions that has a reasoned chance of producing a desired effect.	Strategy	
9. A description of proposed actions.	Action Plan, Strategic plan	
10. The components of an action or strategic plan.	Goals & Objectives, Planned actions	
11. A description of why we think an action or set of actions will work.	Theory of change (Logic model)	
12. A prioritized list of where we need new or better data.	Data Development Agenda	
13. A prioritized list of where we need new information/research about causes and solutions.	Information & Research Agenda	
14. A desired future level of achievement for a population indicator or performance measure.	Target, Goal, Standard, Benchmark	
15. A study or analysis of how well a program is working or has worked.	Program evaluation, Performance evaluation	

(Other modifiers: measurable, urgent, priority, targeted, incremental, systemic, core, quantitative, qualitative, intermediate, ultimate short-term, mid-term, long-term, internal, external, infernal, eternal, allegorical, extraterrestrial)   **FPSI revised Nov 2013**

Appendix C

How Other Planning Terminology Fits with Results-Based Accountability

The word "mission" is usually used in relation to an organization, agency, program, initiative or effort. It is, therefore, mostly used in connection with Performance Accountability. Mission statements are usually concise statements of the purpose of an organization, sometimes also telling why and how the organization does what it does. Mission statements can be useful tools in communicating with internal and external stakeholders. It is possible to construct a mission statement from the performance measures for *How well did we do it?* and *Is anyone better off?* For example:

"Our mission is to help our clients become self sufficient (Is anyone better off?) by providing timely, family-friendly, culturally competent job training services (*How well did we do it?).*

One mistake that organizations often make is to spend months and sometimes years trying to craft the perfect mission statement before any other work is done.[138] In RBA, the task of creating a perfect mission statement can be set aside, allowing the work of identifying and using performance measures to proceed quickly. Later, a small group can craft a workable mission statement using the performance measures as raw material.

The word "vision" is often used to convey the picture of a desired future, one that is hard but possible to attain. This is a powerful idea. One can think of desired results for children, adults, families, and communities as one way to articulate a vision, "We want our community to be one that is safe and supportive, where all children are healthy and ready for school, where all children succeed in school, and grow up to be productive and contributing adults." This is an example of a vision statement made up of at least four different population results. You can craft a vision statement before or after you identify population results.

The word "values" is about what we hold most dear, how we view right and wrong, how we believe we should act, and how those beliefs are reflected in our actions. Our values underlie all of the work we do. That is nowhere more evident than in the work we do on the well-being of children, families, and communities. Our values guide our choice of results for children and families. The actions we take, or fail to take, to improve those results gives tangible meaning to our values. Values Clarification processes sometimes help groups find common ground and work more effectively together.

The word "goal" is sometimes used instead of "result" or "outcome" to label the idea of a condition of well-being for children, adults, families and communities. Georgia, Missouri, and Oregon have a history of using the word "goal" in this way. In the education system, the word "goal" is often used to label important school or student results like, "All children are proficient in reading, writing, math, and science." The word "goal" has many other common usages as well. It often serves as an all-purpose term to describe a desired accomplishment, "my goal for this month is to fix the roof." "Our goal is to increase citizen participation in the planning process."

[138.] See "Get to the Point Planning" in Chapter 4.

"The primary goal of the child welfare system is to keep children safe," and so forth. The words goal and target are sometimes used interchangeably to describe a desired future level of achievement for an indicator or performance measure, "Our goal is 95% high school graduation in 5 years." "Our goal is to improve police response time to under 3 minutes."

Still another use of the word "goal" is in relation to an implementation plan. Given a strategy to improve a particular result, for example, *Children Ready for School*, it is possible to structure the action plan as a series of planned goals with timetables and assigned implementation responsibilities. A typical goal in a *Children Ready for School* plan might be to "increase funding for child care by 10% this year and 20% next year." This is a specific action that will contribute to achieving the result *Children Ready for School.*

These are all widely different usages. Partners must decide which of these ideas will carry the label "goal." Putting a modifier in front of the word goal (such as program goal or service goal) is a way to distinguish different uses of the word. Failure to do this will mean that the word "goal" will have more than one meaning and you will have trouble understanding what people mean when they use the word.

The word "objective" is often paired with the word "goal" to specify a series of "sub-goals" required to achieve the "higher" goal. The terms "mission, goal, and objective" have a long history in the military to describe the strategic and tactical components of an action or engagement. Some of their usage in management and planning processes derives from this history. In RBA, the terms "goal" and "objective" are most often used to structure the action plan and specify who will do what, when, and how.

The words "problem" and "issue" are used in more ways than just about any other planning terms. They can be used to describe almost anything, "The problem with this computer is that the keyboard is too small. The problem with our community is that there is not a safe place for our children to play. We must solve the issue of affordability if we are to provide child care for all who need it." These are three different uses of the words and there are countless others. It can sometimes be helpful to use RBA concepts to figure out what type of problem you have (e.g. high crime rate) and where it fits in the turn the curve thinking process (e.g. need to turn the curve on the population indicator, crime rate).

The words "input" and "output" are commonly used categories for performance measures. The word "input" is most often used to describe the staff and financial resources used by a program to generate "outputs." "Outputs" are most often units of service. Inputs and outputs defined in this way are *How much did we do?* measures. As discussed at the beginning of Chapter 5, the words input and output derive from the industrial tradition of performance measurement, a tradition not well suited to programs that provide services. The three performance measurement categories *How much did we do? How well did we do it? Is anyone better off?* provide a better alternative for service programs.

Appendix D

Framework Crosswalk		
Population Accountability	**Example**	**(framework name)**
1. Population		
2. Results		
3. Indicators		
Data Development Agenda		
4. Baselines		
5. Story behind the baselines		
Info/Research Agenda (causes)		
6. Partners		
7. What works / Strategy		
Info/Research Agenda (solutions)		
8. Action Plan		
9. Budget		
Performance Accountability		
1. Customers		
2. Performance measures		
How much did we do?		
How well did we do it?		
Is anyone better off?		
Data Development Agenda		
3. Baselines		
4. Story behind the baselines		
Info/Research Agenda (causes)		
5. Partners		
6. What works / Strategy		
Program actions		
Partner's actions		
Info/Research Agenda solutions)		
7. Action Plan		
8. Budget		

Appendix E

Turn the Curve Exercise #1 for Population Well-being

Purpose: To provide hands-on experience with results-based decision making at the **population** level. Small groups work on actually "turning the curve" on an indicator of child, adult, family or community well-being. Groups are capable of doing this exercise with little or no advance training in RBA concepts.

Setting up the Exercise

1. Prepare the history part of 3 or more population indicator baselines in advance, or gather the data that will allow the groups to do this. Baseline graphs should allow space on the x axis for forecasting at least 3 years from the present year. If data is not available (or only one point of data is available), the groups can use the technique in Appendix F, "Creating baselines from group knowledge" to create a working version of a baseline. Generally, groups choose which indicator curve they want to work on. In some cases you may want to pre-assign indicators to specific tables or have all the groups work on the same indicator.
2. Give each person a copy of the one-page instruction sheet with time limits for each step, and the group report format. These are shown on page 164, and also appear near the end of the RBA 101 workshop workbook.
3. Participants are asked to work in groups of 4, 5 or 6. You can pre-assign people to groups or let people self select who they want to work with. **For the Population Turn the Curve exercise, it is best if members of the group represent a wide range of perspectives.** There is a natural tendency for people to work with others they know and you may want to discourage this.
4. With a large group you can quickly assemble people into groups using an interesting technique derived from chaos and complexity theory. Announce that "each person is responsible for finding 4 or 5 other people to work with." In just a few minutes most people have formed into a group of the right size, and you can help those who are not in a group find a place. It is important to discourage groups of 8 or more. With groups of this size, some participants will dominate the discussion while others hang back and don't participate. Break these groups up into smaller groups.

Running the Exercise

1. **Starting points** (5 minutes): Each group picks a timekeeper, a reporter, and a geographic area.(Population Accountability is always about a whole population in a geographic area). The reporter will take notes on a regular piece of paper. These notes will be used to produce the group's one-page report on flipchart paper. Each person in the group is asked to wear two hats. The first hat is the hat they wear in their everyday work life. The second hat is the hat of a partner who is not otherwise represented in the group.
2. **Baseline** (10 minutes): Each group picks one of the prepared baselines or constructs a baseline using provided data. If no data is available, the group can construct the history part of the baseline from group knowledge, as noted above. The group agrees on a forecast of where this line is headed if we don't do something "more or different from what we are doing now." This is a crucial step in the exercise, and you should check in with each group, as time permits, to see that this is done correctly. Make sure the groups do **not** plot the

forecast of where they **want** to go. (If you're not careful, this can become a promise. And anything better than baseline will be progress.) Visit tables starting about 10 minutes into the exercise and ask "Can I see your baseline forecast?" With the forecast established, the group asks if this forecasted future is "OK." If the forecast **is** OK, then the group should pick a different baseline to work on. People should work on indicators where there is room for improvement.

3. **Story behind the baseline** (15 minutes): Consider the causes and forces at work. Why does this picture look the way it does? What accounts for the history? Explain the reasoning behind the forecast. (If only 70% of people are successful, who are the 30% who are not, and why?) Keep a list of questions about causes. These questions are the first part of your Information and Research Agenda. Dig deep for causes. Ask "Why?" five times. Don't settle for easy rhetorical answers.

4. **What works?** (What would it take?) (15 minutes): Consider what could work to do better. There are two natural pointers to action. Each cause is a pointer to actions that address that cause, and each partner has something to contribute. Go around the table twice and ask each person what they could contribute wearing each of their two hats. There is only one rule: At least one of the ideas must be a no-cost or low-cost idea. "Sharp edges" means ideas that are specific enough that they can actually be implemented. Keep a list of questions about what works. This is the second part of the Information and Research Agenda.

5. **Report** (10 minutes): Prepare a report on a **single** piece of flipchart paper, using the format shown below. Groups should not get the flipchart paper until the last 10 minutes of the exercise when they are ready to prepare the group's report.

Debriefing the Exercise

1. **Presentations:** You have several options about how the groups report out. 1) The "traditional" method is to have someone from each group come to the front of the room and present to the larger group. People hate this. Don't do this unless you have only two or three groups. 2) Gallery Walk: Have groups post their one page reports on the wall. One person from the group then stays with the report to explain the work, while everyone else tours the work of all the other groups. 3) Modified Gallery Walk: Same as 2) but people are told to visit ONLY ONE report on the wall. With this technique, large groups can get through the report out process in 10 minutes or less.

2. **Questions:** At the end of the exercise and presentations, ask the group: What did you learn from this exercise? How was this experience different from other processes you've worked with in the past? What worked and what didn't? How many people think that a lay audience would understand the one page reports you produced? How many people think they could lead this exercise with a small group? You can also ask the group about the elements of the exercise. Why did we ask for the Forecast? (A forecast that is "not OK" generates a sense of urgency about taking action.) Why did we ask for the Story behind the baseline? (The story is the diagnostic step in the process. The diagnosis of causes points to solutions.) Why did we ask for the No-cost and Low-cost ideas? (It gets us quick wins. We usually don't have new money to work with.) Why did we ask for the Crazy idea? (It gives people permission to be creative and have fun. Remember fun!)

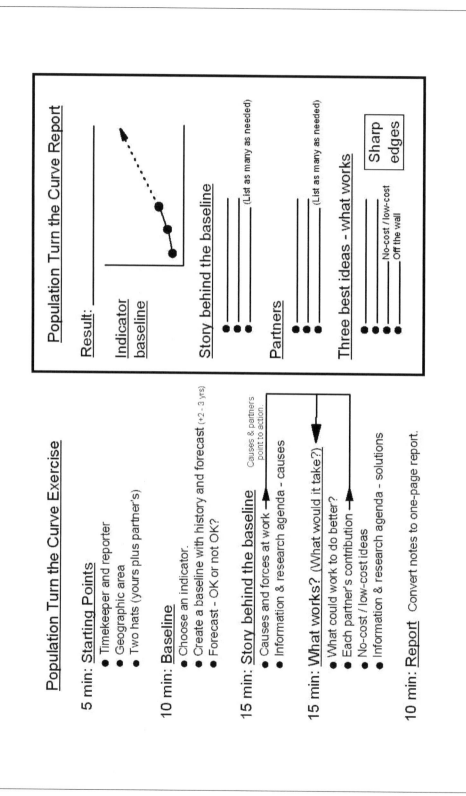

Population Turn the Curve Exercise

5 min: Starting Points
- Timekeeper and reporter
- Geographic area
- Two hats (yours plus partner's)

10 min: Baseline
- Choose an indicator.
- Create a baseline with history and forecast (+2 - 3 yrs)
- Forecast - OK or not OK?

15 min: Story behind the baseline   Causes & partners point to action.
- Causes and forces at work
- Information & research agenda - causes

15 min: What works? (What would it take?)
- What could work to do better?
- Each partner's contribution
- No-cost / low-cost ideas
- Information & research agenda - solutions

10 min: Report   Convert notes to one-page report.

Population Turn the Curve Report

Result: _____

Indicator
baseline

Story behind the baseline

_____
_____
_____   (List as many as needed)

Partners

_____
_____
_____   (List as many as needed)

Three best ideas - what works

_____
_____   No-cost / low-cost
_____   Off the wall

Sharp
edges

Turn the Curve Exercise #2 for Program Performance

Purpose: To provide hands-on experience with results-based decision making at the program **performance** level. Small groups work on actually "turning the curve" on a performance measure for a program. (For participants in the E.U., Australia and New Zealand, substitute the word "service" for "program.") Groups are capable of doing this exercise with little or no advance training in RBA concepts.

Setting up the Exercise

1. If possible, participants should bring data for one or more measures. If participants did not bring data (the more usual case) then show the groups how to use the method in Appendix F, Exercise #3 to construct a working baseline.
2. Give each person a copy of the one-page instruction sheet with time limits for each step and the group report format. These are shown on page 167 and also appear near the end of the RBA 101 workshop workbook.
3. Participants are asked to work in groups of 4, 5 or 6. **For the performance turn the curve exercise it is best for people to work with others from the same service or same organization.** This may sometimes mean groups as small as 3, or even 2.
4. With a large group you can quickly assemble people into groups using an interesting technique derived from chaos and complexity theory. Announce that "each person is responsible for finding 4 or 5 other people to work with." In just a few minutes most people have formed into a group of the right size, and you can help those who are not in a group find a place. It is important to discourage groups of 8 or more. With groups of this size, some participants will dominate the discussion while others hang back and don't participate. Break these groups up into smaller groups.

Running the Exercise

1. **Starting points** (5 minutes): Each group picks a timekeeper and a reporter, and a program to work on. The reporter will take notes on a regular piece of paper. These notes will be used to produce the group's one-page report on flipchart paper. Each person in the group is asked to wear two hats. The first hat is the hat they wear in their everyday work life. The second hat is the hat of a partner who is not otherwise represented at the table.
2. **Baseline** (10 minutes): Each group picks one performance measure from the measures for *How well did we do it?* or *Is anyone better off?* The group constructs a baseline using actual data if possible. If real data is not available, the group can construct a working version of a baseline using the method noted above. The group agrees on a forecast of where this line is headed if we don't do something "more or different from what we are doing now." This is a crucial step in the exercise, and you should check in with each group, as time permits, to see that this is done correctly. Make sure the groups do **not** plot a forecast of where they **want** to go. (If you're not careful, this can become a promise. And anything better than baseline is progress.) Visit tables starting about 10 minutes into the exercise and ask "Can I see the baseline forecast?" With the forecast established, the group asks if this forecasted future is "OK." If the forecast **is** OK, then the group should pick a different baseline to work on. People should work on performance measures where there is room for improvement.
3. **Story behind the baseline** (15 minutes): Consider the causes and forces at work. Why does this picture look the way it does? What accounts for the history? Explain the reason-

ing behind the forecast. (If only 70% of customers are successful, who are the 30% who are not, and why?) Keep a list of questions about causes. These questions are the first part of your Information and Research Agenda. Dig deep for causes. Ask "Why?" five times. Don't settle for easy rhetorical answers.

4. **What works?** (What would it take?) (15 minutes): Consider what could work to do better. There are two natural pointers to action. Each cause is a pointer to actions that address that cause and each partner has something to contribute. Go around the table twice and ask each person what they could contribute wearing each of their two hats. There is only one rule: At least one of the ideas must be a no-cost or low-cost idea. Keep a list of questions about what works. This is the second part of the Information and Research Agenda. "Sharp edges" means that the ideas are specific enough that they can actually be implemented.

5. **Report (10 minutes):** Prepare a report on a single piece of flipchart paper, using the format shown below. Groups should not get the flipchart paper until the last 10 minutes of the exercise when they are ready to prepare the group's report.

Debriefing the Exercise

1. **Presentations:** You have several options about how the groups report out. 1) The "traditional" method is to have someone from each group come to the front of the room and present to the larger group. People hate this. Don't do this unless you have only two or three groups. 2) Gallery Walk: Have groups post their one page reports on the wall. One person from the group then stays with the report to explain the work, while everyone else tours the work of all the other groups. 3) Modified Gallery Walk: Same as 2) but people are told to visit ONLY ONE report on the wall. With this technique, large groups can get through the report out process in 10 minutes or less.

2. **Questions:** At the end of the exercise and presentations, ask the group: What did you learn from this exercise? How was this experience different from other processes you've worked with in the past? What worked and what didn't? How many people think that a lay audience would understand the one page reports you produced? How many people think they could lead this exercise with a small group? You can also ask the group about the elements of the exercise. Why did we ask for the Forecast? (A forecast that is "not OK" generates a sense of urgency about taking action.) Why did we ask for the Story behind the baseline? (The story is the diagnostic step in the process. The diagnosis of causes points to solutions.) Why did we ask for the No-cost and Low-cost ideas? (It gets us quick wins. We usually don't have new money to work with.) Why did we ask for the Crazy idea? (It gives people permission to be creative and have fun. Remember fun!)

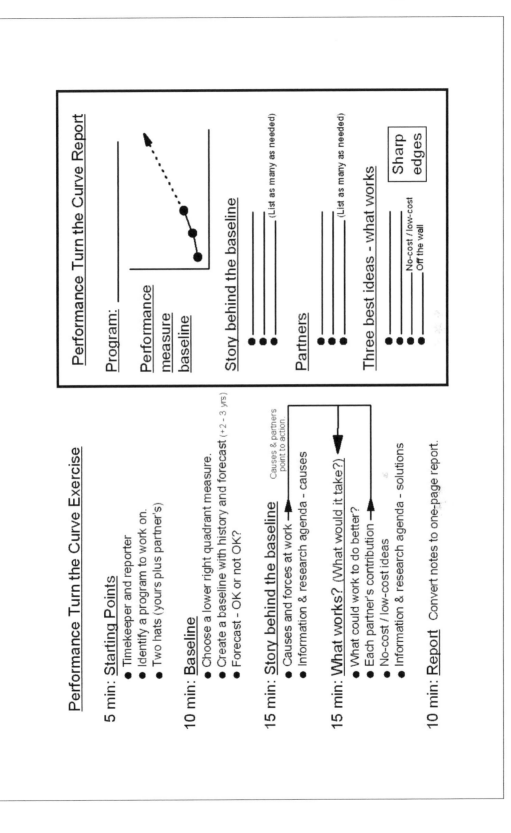

Appendix F

SYNOPSIS OF OTHER RESULTS-BASED ACCOUNTABILITY EXERCISES

The following is a brief description of four other important exercises. The full description of these and other exercises can be found on raguide.org under the Index of Tools, Section A.

1. 20 Minute Performance Exercise: Participants work in pairs. Each pair chooses a program and answers all the Performance Accountability 7 Questions in 20 minutes. This exercise is useful in its own right, but it also answers the objection, "I don't have time to do this."

1. Who are our customers? Identify two customers
2. How can we measure if our customers are better off? Identify one measure.
3. How can we measure if we're delivering services well? Identify one measure.
4. How are we doing on the most important of these measures? Discuss how you're doing on the two measures you identified.
5. Who are the partners with a role to play in doing better? Identify two partners.
6. What works to do better? Identify two "what works" ideas including a no-cost / low-cost idea.
7. What do we propose to do? Discuss how you would implement these two ideas.

2. The Whole Distance Exercise: Put 8 pieces of flipchart paper across the wall, labeled: RESULTS, EXPERIENCE, INDICATORS, BASELINES, STORY, PARTNERS, WHAT WORKS, ACTION PLAN. The facilitator leads the group through each step in the thinking process for one or more results. One nice feature of this exercise is that there are no wrong answers from the group. If a participant suggests a "what works" idea while the group is considering indicators, simply walk down the wall and record the idea on the what works page. The exercise takes about an hour, and can also be used to structure group meetings and public hearings.

3. Creating Baselines from Group Knowledge: When data is not available, or only one point is available, it is still possible to create a working baseline based on group knowledge. Choose an indicator or performance measure to work on. Draw the x/y axes on a piece of paper. In the middle of the x axis write the current year or the word "now." Estimate the current value of the measure. Then ask, "Has this measure been getting better, worse or about the same over the last few years?" (We call this "backcasting.") Draw an increasing, decreasing or flat line history to the current point. Then ask "Where is this measure heading if we don't do anything more or different from what we're doing now?" Draw one or more forecasts from the current point. This baseline can now be used in one of the Turn the Curve Exercises in Appendix E.

4. The Sorting Exercise: This is a fun exercise which involves sorting decks of cards into the correct categories. Each deck takes pieces of a Turn the Curve story and breaks it up into parts. Three card decks are available at raguide.org/results-based-accountability-tools-for-implementation. One card deck addresses an effort to reduce teen pregnancy. Another addresses getting all children ready for school. A third addresses creating a clean environment. Working in small groups, participants write the following categories in order on a single piece of flipchart paper: RESULTS, INDICATORS, BASELINE, TARGET, STORY, PARTNERS, WHAT WORKS and PERFORMANCE MEASURES. The participants paste the cards in the appropriate categories. Remind the group of the definition of "target," a desired future level of achievement for an indicator or performance measure. You can create your own card decks by taking the pieces of any successful turn the curve story. Note that some cards in the online decks can go in more than one category. As discussed in Chapter 5, some performance measures can also double as population indicators. When working with beginners, make sure you edit the card decks so that you only use cards that fit clearly and unambiguously into one category. When the groups are finished, go to each group and check their work. When a card is in the wrong category, ask the group to reconsider the card and agree on a different category. With the whole group, ask "What was the purpose of this exercise?" Answer: When you are doing this work for real, will people give you things in neat categories? No. Your job will be to sort ideas into the correct RBA categories. This makes the turn the curve thinking process possible.

5. **Results List from Scratch**: Create a list of 10 plain language results. Step 1 Ask the participants as a whole group to brainstorm endings to the sentences, "We want children who are...", "We want families that are....", "We want to live in a community that is....". Step 2: Break into three groups (children, families and community). Have each group pare their list of answers down to 5 for children, 3 for families and 2 for the community. Step 3: Bring the large group back together and have each group report their answers. Help the large group make recommendations for changes that will allow the list to function as a whole.

Appendix G

A 5-step method for identifying performance measures for any program in about 45 minutes

In order to identify performance measures, we must first be clear about what part of the organization we are talking about. This can be thought of as a "fence drawing" question. Draw a fence around the agency as a whole or the component program, service, unit or activity whose performance is to be measured. You can also draw a fence around a function, such as supervision, financial management or communications that crosses over lines within the agency. Or you can draw a fence around a group of agencies that make up a service system. As a general rule, it is best to start at the bottom of the organization and identify performance measures for each program or service. These measures can then be used at progressively higher levels of the organization.

The following five step scripted process is the best way to select the most important performance measures and identify a Data Development Agenda for what's inside the fence. With practice, this process can be completed for any program in about 45 minutes.[139] Participants should each have a copy of the performance measurement summary in Figure 4.16.

Step 1. How much did we do? Draw the four quadrants on a piece of flip chart paper. This is best done by sectioning the paper with a vertical and horizontal line. Start in the upper left quadrant. Ask "Who are the customers of this program?" List the different customer groups with a "#" in front of each to signify that we are counting how many of these people we served. For example # of student or # of patients. If there is no special name for the program's customers, simply write down the measure "# of customers." Ask if there are more specific ways to count customers or important subcategories of customers and list them, such as the number of children with disabilities. Most programs have a primary customer. Circle the name of the primary customer. This will be important when we come to the "Is anyone better off?" question below. Note: staff are not customers, unless you are working on internal administrative services.

Next, ask what activities are performed. Convert each activity into a measure. The activity of "training people" becomes #of people trained. Paving roads becomes #of miles of road paved. When you're finished, ask if there are any major activities that are not listed. Don't try to get every last detail, just the most important categories of customers and activities.

Step 2. How well did we do it? Ask people to review the common measures listed in the upper right quadrant of the performance measurement summary (Figure 4.16). Write each one that applies in the upper right quadrant of the flipchart paper.

Next take each activity listed in the upper left quadrant and ask what measures tell how well that particular activity was performed. If you get blank looks, ask if timeliness or accuracy mat-

---

[139]. 45 minutes is an average. Some programs take less time. More complicated programs can take an hour or more. Using the 5-step process is a skill where the speed and the quality of work improves with practice. In large organizations it is often best to work with each service unit across the bottom of the organization chart.

ters. Convert each answer into a measure and be specific. The timeliness of case reviews becomes % of case reviews completed on time. If you are not sure whether a measure goes in the upper right or lower right quadrant, put it where you think best and move on. All the measures in both quadrants will be considered equally in Steps 4 and 5.

Step 3. Is anyone better off? Ask "If your program works really well, how are your customers better off? How are their lives better or different? How could we observe this? How could we measure it?" Create pairs of measures (number and percentage) for each answer. For example, for a job training program, the #of clients who get jobs goes in the lower left quadrant. And the % of clients who get jobs goes in the lower right quadrant. It saves time, when entering these measures, to write them only once in the lower right quadrant, and place # signs in the lower left quadrant across from each measure. For programs that manage infrastructure (e.g. roads, bridges, water and sewer systems) the infrastructure itself can be considered a customer for purposes of this question. So for example #/% of roads or bridges rated in good (or poor) condition, or #/rate of water main breaks.

Identifying whether anyone is better off is the most interesting and challenging part of this process. Dig deep into the different ways in which service benefits show up in the lives of the people served. Explore each of the four categories of better-offness: Skills / Knowledge, Attitude / Opinion, Behavior, and Circumstance. If people get stuck, try the reverse question: "If your service didn't work, how would your customers be worse off? How would it show up in their lives?"

Look first for data that is already collected. Then be creative about things that could be counted and how the data could be generated. It is not always necessary to have data for all of your customers. Data based on samples can be used. Pre and post testing can be used to show improvement over time in skills, knowledge, attitude and opinion. When no other data is available, ask clients to self report about improvements or benefits.

Keep in mind that all data have two incarnations: a lay definition and a technical definition. The lay definition is something that everyone can understand. The technical definition gives the exact way in which the measure is constructed. For example, "high school graduation rate" is a lay definition with many possible technical definitions. The easiest technical definition is the number who graduate as a percentage of enrollment one month before graduation. This will always be close to

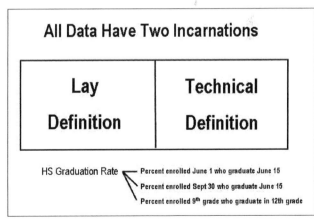

100%. A tougher technical definition would compare graduation numbers to enrollment at the beginning of the school year. A still tougher definition would compare graduation to the enrollment three or four years earlier. Each technical definition constitutes a **separate measure**.

When you complete step 3, you will have filled in the four quadrants with as many entries as possible. In steps 4 and 5, we use a shortcut method to assess the communication, proxy and data power of each measure and winnow these down to the most important measures.

Step 4. Headline measures: Review the list of upper right and lower right quadrant measures and identify those for which there is good data. By good data we mean that timely and reliable data for the measure is available **today** or could be produced within an hour.If the data is in the system somewhere, but it would take you more than an hour to aggregate it then you don't have it. Put a circle next to each one of these measures. Next, ask "If you had to talk about the performance of your program in a public setting, such as a presentation to elected officials or a presentation at a public hearing or conference, and you could use only **one** of the measures with a circle, which one would you choose?" Put a "#1" by the answer. Then ask "If you could have a second measure... and a third?" You should identify no more than 3 to 5 measures. These should be a mix of upper right and lower right measures. These choices represent a working list of headline measures for the program.

Step 5. Data Development Agenda: Ask, "If you could buy one of the measures for which you don't have data, the ones without the circles, which one would it be?" The word "buy" is used because data is expensive both in terms of money and worker time. With a different colored marker, write DDA #1 next to the chosen measure. "If you could buy a second measure... and a third?" List no more than 3 to 5 measures. These measures are the program's Data Development Agenda in priority order.

This process leads to a three part list of performance measures:

> **Headline measures**: Those 3 to 5 most important measures for which you have good data, the measures you would use to present your program's performance in a public setting.

> **Secondary measures**: All other measures for which you now have good data. These measures will be used to help manage the program, and will often figure in the story behind the headline measure baselines.

> **Data Development Agenda**: A prioritized list of measures where you need new or better data. You will later need to make a judgment about how far down this list you can afford to go.

Appendix H

More Performance Measurement Examples
(supplementary to those given in Chapter 4)

Program	How well did we do it?	Is anyone better off?
Welfare to Work	Percent of trainees who complete job training program, unit cost per trainee.	Percent of trainees who get jobs paying a living wage with benefits, Percent who still have jobs 6 and 12 months later.
Child Welfare	Ratio of workers to foster children, Ratio of workers to child abuse / neglect cases, Percent of children with multiple placements in the last 6 months, Percent of siblings placed together, Percent of foster children placed in same school catchment area.	Percent of foster children with good school attendance, Percent of foster children reunified or in permanent placement within 6 months of entering care, Rate of repeat child abuse or child neglect.
Juvenile Justice	Percent in community based vs. institutional care, Percent of intake screenings on time, Ratio of youth to probation officers, Occupancy rate for Juvenile Hall.	Recidivism rate, Percent exiting custody with no repeat offense in 6, 12, 24 months, Rate of probation violation, Percent of youth in school or jobs 6, 12 months after exit.
Adult Corrections	Inmate/staff ratio, Percent of positive drug screenings, Rate of disruptive incidents per month, Percent of inmates receiving drug treatment, Percent of inmates receiving mental health services.	Rate of escapes, Rate of recidivism, Percent of inmates who get and keep jobs 6, 12 months after release.
Transportation	Percent of maintenance on schedule, fuel consumption efficiency, transit boardings, transit revenue as % of operating costs	Percent of roads and bridges in good condition, inter-regional corridor travel speed, % transit on schedule, Disability compliance (Note: traffic fatalities and modal split are population indicators)
Mental Health	Waiting list size, Average time to next open appointment.	Percent of clients in school or working, Rate of entry into institutional care, Rate of movement to less restrictive care.
Public Housing	Vacancy rate, Percent tenants paying rent on time.	Percent tenants who transition to non-subsidized housing, Percent tenants satisfied with building maintenance.
Education	Retention rate for highly qualified teachers, Percent of teachers with degrees in the subject they are teaching.	High school graduation rate, Percent of students with good attendance, Percent proficient or better at reading, writing, math and science by grade level.

Program	How well did we do it?	Is anyone better off?
Special Education	Rate of disproportional representation of minorities, Percent of special education students in mainstream classrooms.	Attendance rate, Graduation rate, Percent of parents who think the school is doing a good job preparing their child for life.
Economic Development	Ranking on "business friendly" environment, Average time from inquiry to response.	Rate of job growth from new businesses. Rate of living wage job growth, Percent of jurisdiction revenues paid by businesses.
Advocacy organization	Percent of targeted policy makers contacted.	Percent of advocacy agenda adopted, Percent of all potential policy makers who have adopted advocated policy.
Research organization	Percent of projects on schedule and on budget.	Rate of citations for published research, Percent of research that leads to market application in 2 to 5 years, Percent of practitioners using findings, For medical research, percent of research that goes to stage III (human testing) trials.
Foundation or Funder	Percent of grants awarded on time, Percent of payments to grantees and vendors within 30 days of invoice, Percent of grants developed and presented using a results framework.	Percent of grantees that report progress on customer results, Percent of grantees that can demonstrate a turned curve related to funder investment.

Administrative Service	How well did we do it?	Is anyone better off?
Human Resources (HR)	Percent of vacancies filled (or offers made) within 30 / 60 / 90 days.	Rate of non-promotional turnover, Percent of supervisory staff who report that HR provides the support they need to do their jobs (customer satisfaction).
Professional Development	Percent of staff with professional development plans, Percent pf positive evaluations for staff development workshops.	Percent who report applying new learning 6 months after training, Percent who report that professional development helped them do a better job.
Information Systems	Percent of system uptime during business hours, Percent of responses to requests for help in less than 24 hours, Percent of projects on time and on budget, Ratio of entry MIS salary to area labor market average (competitive salaries).	Percent of staff who report that MIS provides the support they need to do their jobs (customer satisfaction).

Administrative Service	How well did we do it?	Is anyone better off?
Building Services	Percent of responses to building services requests / reports in less than 24 hours, Facility maintenance cost per square foot, Ratio of actual to budgeted building operations costs.	Percent of occupants satisfied that the building environment meets their needs and adequately supports their job performance (customer satisfaction).
Legal Counsel	Number of lawsuits against the agency per year, number of written opinions/advice.	Percent of lawsuits successfully litigated, Percent settled out of court, Percent of successful appeals, Percent of senior staff who report that counsel provides the support they need to do their jobs (customer satisfaction).
Budget and Finance	Percent of invoices paid in 30 days, Percent of report submissions on time, Budget surplus or deficit. Unit cost, Administrative cost overhead rate, Percent increase or decrease in budgeted or actual cost.	Percent of repeat audit findings, Percent of senior staff who report that budget and finance provides the support they need to do their jobs (customer satisfaction). Surplus / deficit - in total and as percent of the total budget, Approved budget as percent of requested budget.
Audit	Percent of audits on schedule.	Rate of repeat findings, Dollar value of corrected audit findings.as % of agency total budget.
Public Information	Rate of website visitors and hits per month.	Rate of repeat visitors to website, Rate of positive press coverage, Percent of staff who report that they are satisfied with internal communications, with press coverage and with the public image of the organization (customer satisfaction).
Executive Office	Percent of units or offices personally visited.	Director's performance rating by the Board, Percent of staff with "good" morale (sometimes framed as answers to the question "Is this a good place to work? or "Do you feel you get the support you need to do your best work?"), Percent of budget requests approved, Percent of fund raising goals met. An interesting composite measure for agencies that have established headline performance measures throughout the organization: Percent of all headline performance measures headed in the right direction.

Appendix I

A SIMPLE FINANCING SELF ASSESSMENT

Questions to Answer about Financing an Agenda to Improve Results for Children and Families...and Other Action Agendas

HOW TO USE THIS SELF ASSESSMENT QUESTIONNAIRE: List each element of your action plan down the left side of a sheet. For **each** element that needs to be funded, ask **all** of the following questions. Make notes on the right side of the sheet about any financing approaches that look possible. Assign follow-up responsibility to gather more information or to take action on promising approaches.

A. **REDEPLOYMENT**: Using the resources already in the system.

1. **Return on investment**: Where do the savings from our activities show up? Can we get our hands on those savings? For example, family support centers increase the immunization rate and decrease Medicaid utilization; family preservation services decrease foster care entries and costs. Approach those organizations that stand to benefit and ask for a share of their savings.

2. **Capitation**: Can we take the money in a package, instead of many individual streams and use money more flexibly across categorical boundaries to fund prevention services?

3. **Cuts**: Can we cut something that isn't working so well to fund something that is? Can we shave small amounts from lots of places to generate resources for something new? For example, the state of Pennsylvania cut one percent from a wide range of programs to fund the first 27 family support centers

4. **Material**: Can we use non-monetary resources (such as people, space, equipment) to meet the needs of our plan? Can we barter for things we need?

B. **REVENUE**: Finding new resources.

1. **Open-ended federal funds**: These are sometimes referred to as entitlement funds. The federal government is obligated to pay all valid state claims. Can we tap into one of the remaining open-ended federal fund sources to pay for part of our plan?

   a. **There are two ways to do this**:

   Directly: Pay for the planned service directly with federal funds and non-federal matching funds

   Indirectly: This is sometimes called "refinancing." Use open-ended federal funds to pay for something that is now paid with 100% state and/or local funds, freeing those funds for reinvestment.

b. **There are two principle open-ended federal fund sources** that can be used in this way. Each can pay for services and for broadly defined "administrative" activities: Title IV-E: Foster Care and Subsidized Adoption, and Title XIX: Medicaid. Note that these fund sources can be politically and technically hard to access.

2. **Capped federal funds**: How can we get a share of capped categorical federal grant funds? These are usually fully spoken for, but the best places to look include:

   a. **Funds which are increasing**: It's always easier to get a share of new money than to fight for someone else's current funding. Do your research on what's going up whether it is Head Start, Immunization, School to Work, or Family Preservation and Support Act funds

   b. **Funds with (new) flexibility regarding use**: Changes in federal education law make some funding sources such as Education's Title I more flexible. Welfare reform has made employment and child care funding more flexible; Waivers (like those used in the Oregon Option) have combined funding streams.

   c. **Funds which are competitive**: Many federal grants are awarded competitively, either directly by the federal government or through the states such as child abuse prevention grants, family support grants, community schools. There are thousands of these grants awarded every year.

3. **State and Local Funds**:

   a. **Fair share of revenue growth**: How can we assure that children get their "fair share" of growth in state and local funding and are protected in a fair way from cuts? Children's Budgets such as those in Los Angeles, Oklahoma and Kansas can help make the case.

   b. **Competitive grants**: Are there state or local grant programs that can be used to fund the agenda? States often have their own programs such as state-only family support or child care programs.

4. **Private Funding**:

   a. **Donations**: Who are our current and potential partners? How can they help? It is important to consider businesses, foundations, and private citizens For example, one family support center in Baltimore had over 300 donors on its list.

   b. **Fees**: Even small (sliding scale) charges can help.

   c. **Third party collections**: Someone else may be obligated to pay for this such as health or other insurance carriers.

   d. **Loans**: Loans may help with program start-up funding or help community agencies get needed credit. Consider banks and other financing institutions such community development corporations. "Bridge financing" can help projects, such as low income housing development, to cover costs until revenues are sufficient to sustain operations.

5. **Politics and Grantsmanship**: Money is politics. Use your connections. Hire someone full time or part time to go after grants. Fund development positions almost always pay for themselves many times over.

C. **RESTRUCTURING**: Changing the structures and incentives that drive the use of money.

1. **Fund pools**: Package prevention and remediation dollars together to create an incentive to save on remediation and invest in prevention. This is the idea behind managed care and Iowa's Decategorization program. Fund pools work best when they are virtual, not actual. (See pages 32-33.)

2. **Flexible dollars**: Examine whether it is possible to change the rules to allow workers to use small amounts of money flexibly to respond to family needs.

3. **Incentives**: Explore whether incentives can be changed to drive resources to desired purposes.

Appendix J

Selected Readings and Resources

BOOKS:

Chaos: Making a New Science, James Gleick, Penguin Books, 1987

Within Our Reach: Breaking the Cycle of Disadvantage, Lisbeth Schorr, Doubleday, 1988.

Complexity: The Emerging Science at the Edge of Order and Chaos, M. Mitchell Waldrop, Simon and Schuster, 1992.

Out of Control: The New Biology of Machines, Social Systems and the Economic World, Kevin Kelly, Perseus Books, 1994.

The Universe and the Teacup: The Mathematics of Truth and Beauty, K.C. Cole, Harcourt Brace and & Company, 1997.

Common Purpose: Strengthening Families and Neighborhoods to Rebuild America, Lisbeth Schorr, Doubleday, 1997.

The Tipping Point: How Little Things Can Make a Big Difference, Malcolm Gladwell, Back Bay Books, Little Brown and Co., 2000.

Poor Economics: A Radical Rethinking of the Way to Fight Global Poverty, Public Affairs, Abhijit Banerjee, Esther Duflo, 2012

Results Based Facilitation: Moving From Talk to Action, (Vols: Introduction, Foundation Skills, Advanced Skills), Sherbrooke Consulting Inc., Jolie Bain Pillsbury, 2013.

The Holy Grail of Public Leadership: And the Never-Ending Quest for Measurable Impact, Fourth Quadrant Publishing, Adam Luecking, 2013.

Who Is Driving The Bus: One Legislator's Road to Accountability, Fourth Quadrant Publishing, Diana S. Urban, 2014.

Stop Spinning Your Wheels: Using RBA to Steer Your Agency To Success, Fourth Quadrant Publishing, Anne McIntyre-Lahner, 2015.

Turning Curves: An Accountability Companion Reader, Mark Friedman, PARSE, 2015.

PAPERS:

The Cosmology of Financing: Financing Reform of Family and Children's Services: An Approach to the Systematic Consideration of Financing Options, Mark Friedman, The Center for the Study of Social Policy, 1994.

From Outcomes to Budgets: An Approach to Outcomes Based Budgeting for Family and Children's Services, Center for the Study of Social Policy, Mark Friedman, 1995.

The Future of Our Children: Long-term Outcomes of Early Childhood Programs, Center for the Future of Children, The David and Lucile Packard Foundation, Volume 5, Number 3, futureofchildren.org, Winter, 1995.

A Strategy Map for Results-based Budgeting: Moving from Theory to Practice, Mark Friedman, The Finance Project, September, 1996.

A Guide to Selecting Results and Indicators, Atelia I. Melaville, The Finance Project, May, 1997.

A Guide to Developing and Using Performance Measures in Results-Based Budgeting, Mark Friedman, The Finance Project, 1997.

A Guide to Developing and Using Family and Children's Budgets, Mark Friedman and Anna Danegger, The Finance Project, 1998.

Capturing Cash for Kids: A Workbook for Reinvesting in Community Based Prevention Approaches for Children and Families, The Comprehensive Integrated Services Reinvestment Project, Marty Giffin, Abram Rosenblatt, Nancy Mills and Mark Friedman, The Foundation Consortium for California's Children and Youth, 1998.

New Approaches to Evaluating Community Initiatives, Edited by Karen Fulbright-Anderson, Anne C. Kubisch, and James P. Connell, The Aspen Institute, 1998.

Reforming Finance, Financing Reform for Family and Children's Services, What Works Policy Brief, The Foundation Consortium for California's Children and Youth, Mark Friedman, January, 2000.

Results-Based Grantmaking: An Approach to Decision Making for Foundations and Other Funders, Mark Friedman, Fiscal Policy Studies Institute, October, 2000.

Results-Based Accountability for Proposition 10 Commissions: A Planning Guide for Improving the Well-Being of Young Children and Their Families, Mark Friedman, The UCLA Center for Healthier Children, Families and Communities, March, 2000.

Getting to Results: Data-Driven Decision-Making for Children, Youth, Families and Communities, What Works Policy Brief, Jacqueline McCroskey, PhD, The Foundation Consortium for California's Children and Youth, 2000.

Toward An Economics of Prevention: Illustrations from Vermont's Experience, Cornelius D. Hogan and David A. Murphey, Finance Project, December, 2000.

Informed Consent: Advice for State and Local Leaders on Implementing Results-Based Decision-making, Sara Watson, Finance Project, 2000.

Improving Children's Lives: A Tool Kit for Positive Results, Susan Robison, National Conference of State Legislatures, 2001.

Evaluation Methodology, Harvard Family Research Project *Evaluation Exchange,* Volume XI, No. 2, Summer, 2005.

Working Together to Improve Results: Reviewing the Effectiveness of Community Decision-Making Entities, Phyllis Brunson and partners, Center for the Study of Social Policy, 2006.

Turning Curves, Achieving Results: A Report of the Annie E. Casey Foundation's Children and Family Fellowship, Molly McGrath, Craig Levine, Brenda Donald, Dennis Campa, Yolie Flores Aguilar, AECF, 2007.

Better Outcomes for Children and Young People - From Talk to Action: UK Department for Children, Schools and Families, David Utting principle author, Crown Copyright, 2008.

ResultStat(tm): Driving Better Government Decisions with Data, Mark Friedman, Phil Lee, Adam Luecking and Andrew Boyd, Results Leadership Group, 2009.

Cardiff: What Matters: 2010:2020 - The 10 Year Strategy, Consultation Draft, December 2010.

Evaluation of Results-Based Accountability, Chronic Conditions Management Demonstrators Evaluation Report, prepared for the NHS Wales by Opinion Research Services (ccmdemonstrators.com), May 2011.

Key Indicator Systems: Experiences of Other National and Subnational Systems Offer Insights for the United States, US Government Accountability Office, Principle author Bernice Steinhardt, 2011.

What's Wrong With Logic Models, NSW Local Community Services Association (LCSA), Occasional Paper No. 1, Phil Lee, 2011.

Expanding the Evidence Universe, Lisbeth Schorr and Frank Farrow, Center for the Study of Social Policy, 2011.

Thought Exercises on Accountability and Performance Measures at the National Heart,Lung and Blood Institute (NHLBI): An Invited Commentary for Circulation Research, *Circulation Research*, American Heart Association, Circ. Res. 2011:108;405-409, 2011.

Results-Based Accountability: The road to better results: Targeting Capacity Building and Philanthropic Partnerships, Annie E. Casey Foundation, Phyllis Rozansky

The Vermont Accountability Compact, Benchmarks for Better Vermont and the Vermont Accountability Group, bbvt.marlboro.edu/#!compact/c185r, 2012.

Outcomes Project - Final Evaluation Report, Social Services Improvement Agency (SSIA), CordisBright Consulting Agency, 2013, check on line for final version and publication date.

Outcomes Based Accountability in Leeds: 'What is it like to be a child or young person in Leeds... And how do we make it better,' 2013

Next Generation Contracting: A Contract Reform Agenda for Funders and Nonprofits, Fiscal Policy Studies Institute, Mark Friedman, 2013.

The Collective Impact Toolkit, Results Leadership Group, Justin Miklas, 2013.

Achieving Collective Impact with Results-Based Accountability, Results Leadership Group, Deitre Epps 2013.

Measuring Results in the Real World: A better way to link policy analysis and performance management: Mark Funkhouser, *Governing Magazine*, March, 2014.

Ten changes to reinvigorate children's social work, The Guardian, Andy Gill, 2014

A Community Partnership Planning Resource, The Government of South Australia, Department for Education and Child Development, www.decd.sa.gov.au/cpp/files/links/cppr_2014_v8.pdf, 2014.

An Evidence Framework to Improve Results, Lisbeth Schorr, Frank Farrow, Joshua Sparrow, Center for the Study of Social Policy, 2014.

Outcomes Based Accountability (in) Essex County Council, Strategy and Communications, Chelmsford, Essex, UK, 2014.

Collective Impact Using RBA, Fiscal Policy Studies Institute, Mark Friedman, 2014.

New Ways of Using Data in Federal Place-Based Initiatives: Opportunities to Create a Results Framework and Raise the Visibility of Equity Issues, Victor Rubin & Michael McAfee, whatcountsforamerica.org, 2014.

Evaluation of Core Assets Support Programme: Using an Outcomes-Based Approach Making a difference to the life of Merthyr Tydfil's children and young people, Merthyr Tydfil Borough Council, (including contributions from Core Assets and Rob Hutchinson), March 2015 (search on line for final report).

How to Achieve the Performance Imperative with Results-Based Accountability, Results Leadership Group, Adam Luecking 2015.

WEBSITES:

Accelerate Performance: accelerateperformance.co.za

Annie E. Casey Foundation: aecf.org

Center for the Study of Social Policy: cssp.org

Child Trends: childtrends.org

Coalition for Evidence-Based Policy: evidencebasedpolicy.org

Finance Project: financeproject.org

Fiscal Policy Studies Institute: raguide.org and resultsaccountability.com

Forum for Youth Investment: forumforyouthinvestment.org

Higherlife Foundation: higherlifefoundation.com

Institute for Educational Leadership: iel.org

National Center for Children in Poverty: childcareresearch.org

Northern Ireland National Children's Bureau: ncb.org.uk/who-we-are/northern-ireland

NGA Center for Best Practices: nga.org/CBP/center.asp

Pathways to Outcomes: pathwaystooutcomes.org

Policy Link: policylink.org

Promising Practices Network: promisingpractices.net

RBA/OBA Facebook Group: www.facebook.com/groups/RBAOBA

Results Leadership Group: resultsleadership.org

Results Leadership Group Australia: resultsleadership.org.au

Safe Youth: safeyouth.org

Search Institute: search-institute.org

University of Maryland School of Public Policy: publicpolicy.umd.edu

Urban Institute: urban.org

UK Resources: davidburnby.co.uk/resources

OTHER RESOURCES:

Results-Based Accountability 101 Powerpoint Presentation: The complete Powerpoint presentation used in the basic 3 hour workshop on Results-Based Accountability 101 can be downloaded for free from resultsaccountability.com/workshops/materials/. The 45 page handout material that goes with the workshop can also be printed from this site. Use these materials to create your own presentation on Results-Based Accountability for your partners or coworkers (If you do this, please make sure you provide attribution. See also the notes at the end of Chapter 9).

Training for Trainers and Coaches: The Fiscal Policy Studies Institute and the Results Leadership Group offer training for those who wish to learn how to teach and coach Results-Based Accountability. These classes are offered from time to time and enrollment is limited. Future class announcements are posted to the website resultsaccountability.com.

The Results Scorecard is a powerful decision-making support software developed by the Results Leadership Group in 2010. It is designed to help non-profits and government agencies implement the RBA framework and create measurable collective impact for organizations and communities. It does so by connecting stakeholders in a single, interactive network, providing rapid access to data, and creating visual dashboards that can be used to improve decision-making and accelerate the RBA Talk-to-Action process. The software uses a simple and intuitive design, and the language can be customized to support each organization's unique terminology. Individuals interested in trying the Results Scorecard can sign up for a free trial at www.resultsscorecard.com.

VIDEO:

Building a Results-Based Accountability Framework: Video of the July 19, 1999 California Teleconference Presentation for Prop 10 (First 5) Commissions, with an introduction by Rob Reiner, sponsored by the California Children and Families First (First 5) State Commission, The California Endowment and the Foundation Consortium for California's Children and Youth. Copies available from the Fiscal Policy Studies Institute.

Results-Based Accountability 101 DVD: Full RBA 101 presentation by Mark Friedman (2.5 hours)- available from the Results Leadership Group - ordering information at resultsleadership.org.

RBA 101 Presentation to the Ontario Local Immigration Partnerships (LIPs) Conference, Toronto, Canada, youtube.com/watch?v=OsKb9YRxgt4, 2012.

Common Good Vermont: Vermont Nonprofit Legislative Day 2013: Mark Friedman on Results-Based Accountability, cctv.org/tags/rba.

Mark Friedman Discusses Results-Based Accountability™ on CNBC Africa, resultsleadership.org/mark-friedman-discusses-rba-cnbc-africa, October, 2014.

Index

Made in the USA
San Bernardino, CA
21 January 2018